MY HERO

by
Fred McMane
and
Cathrine Wolf

A *Sports Illustrated For Kids* Book

BANTAM BOOKS

TORONTO • NEW YORK • LONDON • SYDNEY • AUCKLAND

My Hero by Fred McMane and Cathrine Wolf

A Bantam Book/July 1994

Sports Illustrated For Kids and **KIDS** are registered trademarks of Time Inc.
Sports Illustrated For Kids Books are published in cooperation with Bantam
Doubleday Dell Publishing Group, Inc. under license from Time Inc.

Cover and interior design by Miriam Dustin

ISBN 0-553-48164-9

Published simultaneously in the United States and Canada

Bantam books are published by Bantam Books, a division of Bantam Doubleday
Dell Publishing Group, Inc. Its trademark, consisting of the words "Bantam Books"
and the portrayal of a rooster, is Registered in the U.S. Patent and Trademark
Office and in other countries. Marca Registrada. Bantam Books, 1540 Broadway,
New York, NY 10036

Printed in the United States of America

CWO 10 9 8 7 6 5 4 3 2

★ TABLE OF CONTENTS ★

DEDICATION

To our daughters,
Sarah, Emily, and Kelly,
who enrich our lives with their
daily gifts of tenderness, generosity,
and laughter.
May they provide heroic inspiration
to future generations.

INTRODUCTION

Whether we realize it or not, our lives are shaped by the people we most admire. Those people might include a family member, a teacher, a doctor, or someone we admire from afar. Our heroes come in different shapes and sizes, but, in our eyes, they are all 10 feet tall.

Sports stars are natural heroes for many of us because they have great physical talents and show courage and coolness under pressure. We are dazzled by their successes, and we study the way they handle failures and difficulties. We are inspired by them to try to set high standards for ourselves.

"I have always had standards and values," said Chris Evert, the former tennis champion. "In my public life as well as my private life. I have always understood the need for heroes." Chris, of course, is a hero herself to many young players.

In this book, we have profiled 10 of today's leading athletes and the sports heroes they admired when they were growing up. The hero often had such an impact that the younger athlete grew up to be a lot like his or her hero. Is it by chance that Cal Ripken, Junior of the Baltimore Orioles has a similar playing record, easy-going demeanor, and social consciousness of his hero, Brooks Robinson? Did Scottie Pippen just happen to become a smooth, high-flying forward like his hero, Julius Erving?

Not likely. It's important to have heroes, and for many of the people in this book, it's important to be on the other side, too. "When you ask me if it's important to have been a hero," Chris Evert once said, "I say, 'Yes, it is.'"

CHAPTER ONE

SCOTTIE PIPPEN
AND HIS HERO:
★ JULIUS ERVING ★

It wasn't easy to play in the shadow of Michael Jordan, much less establish yourself as a star in your own right. But that is exactly what forward Scottie Pippen of the Chicago Bulls did. Scottie displayed his unique skills and style in helping the Bulls win three National Basketball Association (NBA) championships in a row from 1991 through 1993.

Scottie is one of the best defensive forwards in the NBA. During his first six years in the league, through the 1992–93 season, he averaged 16.1 points and 6.6 rebounds per game. Like Michael and nine other NBA stars, Scottie was a member of the "Dream Team," the basketball team representing the United States that won the gold medal in the 1992 Summer Olympics in Barcelona, Spain.

It's quite amazing that Scottie has achieved so much in basketball because, as a kid growing up in Hamburg, Arkansas, he wasn't an exceptional player. He made his high school varsity basketball team in 10th grade, but he spent the whole season on the bench. Even at the start of the next season he wasn't allowed to play in games. That was because he skipped the basketball team's weightlifting sessions during the fall to become

As a kid, Scottie didn't show great promise as a basketball player. Now he's an NBA All-Star!

manager of the school's football team instead!

"I love football," said Scottie. "It was never my sport to play, but I enjoy watching, and I wanted to be around the game."

Midway through the season, the basketball coach gave in and allowed Scottie to play a little. By his senior year, Scottie had become the team's starting shooting guard—in large part because the coach needed players!

"Mostly everyone else had graduated," Scottie said.

Because he was a skinny kid, Scottie had to rely more on

good ball-handling skills than on power. In his senior year, the team won more than 20 games and went on to the regionals of the state championship tournament.

Still, no college offered Scottie a scholarship. Instead, his high school coach helped him get a work-study grant to be manager of the basketball team at the University of Central Arkansas. This grant provided him with money for school.

Scottie made the most of the opportunity. He lifted weights before the season started and played pickup ball with the guys from the team. He also began to grow taller.

When Scottie arrived at Central Arkansas, the basketball coach told him he might be able to make the team in a year or two if he got bigger and stronger. But when several players quit the team, Scottie got a chance to play sooner than expected.

He averaged only 4.3 points per game in his first varsity season, but he showed a lot of heart and hustle. He also grew to 6' 7" and got a chance to play every position— guard, forward, and center.

Scottie developed great skills on both offense and defense. During his senior season, he was the best college player in the state of Arkansas. He averaged 23.6 points and nearly 10 rebounds per game. The professional scouts, however, were not impressed because Central Arkansas did not play top-notch college teams. The scouts were not sure Scottie could handle the competition of pro basketball.

Scottie believed in himself, though. "I knew deep down that I could do well," he told *Sports Illustrated For Kids* magazine. "I had skills that I hadn't seen in players my size, and I knew I could work that to my advantage."

Scottie went to a tryout camp for the pros and stole the show. The Seattle SuperSonics selected him fifth in the NBA Draft, then traded him to Chicago, where he would play with His Airness.

Scottie is now one of the most exciting players in the NBA. Watching him glide through the air for one of his exciting dunks, fans are sometimes reminded of Julius Erving, a star player during the 1970's and 1980's. That's no coincidence. As a kid playing on the playground, Scottie used to fantasize about being Doctor J.

SCOTTIE SAYS: "A lot of people say I remind them of Julius. I always wanted to play like him and be like him."

"I would be on the court daydreaming that I was Julius Erving," said Scottie. "It would be the last game of the championship series. I had the ball, and I was taking the last shot of the game.

"[Doctor J] was somebody I looked up to and admired. I just liked his personality on and off the court. I respected his game, the way he played it, the way he spoke. He had a very positive attitude. He was one of those people you wanted to be like."

Scottie got to meet Doctor J in 1991 at the Naismith Memorial Basketball Hall of Fame in Springfield, Massachusetts. "I talked to him a little, shook his hand, and took a picture with him," Scottie recalls. "It was just like a dream come true to have an opportunity to meet him."

It's not really surprising that a star like Scottie would feel that way. After all, Julius Erving was one of the most exciting players ever to step onto a basketball court.

★ JULIUS ERVING ★

Julius Erving did not invent the dunk shot, but he did more than any other basketball player in history to turn it into an art form. Before all the incredible dunkers of today, Doctor J, as Julius was called, was flying through the air, seeming to defy gravity. Basketball fans had never seen anything like it before.

Julius had great physical gifts: He was 6' 6½" tall, with tremendous leaping ability and huge hands. He could rebound, as well as shoot the ball. In college, at the University of Massachusetts, he averaged more than 26 points and 20 rebounds a game! He was a tough competitor, too, but he rarely showed that toughness with words or gestures. He let his abilities do the talking for him.

And they spoke loud and clear: During his 16-year career as a pro, Julius led his teams to three championships and was named Most Valuable Player (MVP) in both the American Basketball Association (ABA) and the NBA. He finished his career with 30,026 points. Only superstar centers Kareem Abdul-Jabbar (38,387) and Wilt Chamberlain (31,419) scored more, as of the start of the 1993–94 season.

It isn't the titles, honors, and records, though, that basketball fans remember most about Doctor J. It's his creativity on the court—his acrobatic dunks and impossible passes—that made him really special.

Julius Winfield Erving II was born on February 22, 1950, in Hempstead, New York. Hempstead is located on Long Island, not far from New York City. When he was three years old, his dad abandoned the family. Julius's mom, Callie, took on the task of raising Julius, his older sister, Alexis, and his younger brother, Marvin. Mrs. Erving worked cleaning houses and collected welfare, but there was never a lot of money around the Erving home.

Julius was a quiet, serious kid, but obviously a very talented one on the basketball court. By the time he was 11, he was 5' 6" tall and had hands as big as any grown man's. He also had so much spring in his legs that he could rebound as well as

Doctor J was the original Dunkmeister who seemed able to beat gravity, as well as his opponents.

HEINZ KLUETMEIER/SPORTS ILLUSTRATED

kids who were 6 feet tall. He dunked a basketball for the first time when he was in sixth grade!

From ages 10 to 12, Julius played on a youth team that was sponsored by the local Salvation Army Center. The team was very good and traveled all over Long Island and as far as Pennsylvania to play games.

The summer before Julius entered eighth grade, his mother remarried and the family moved to Roosevelt, another community on Long Island. Julius spent hours playing playground basketball, learning to play well—and with style. Soon he was also starring for the school teams at Roosevelt Junior-Senior High.

Name: Julius Winfield Erving II
Nickname: Doctor J
Born: February 22, 1950, Hempstead, New York
Height: 6' 6½"
Weight: 200 pounds
Cool fact: Julius is the only player to win the slam dunk championships in both the National Basketball Association and the American Basketball Association.

It was during his years at Roosevelt High School that Julius picked up his nickname. It was clear that he was such an expert in his field (basketball) that the other kids started calling him Doctor. Later, during a summer league game, the public address announcer was struggling to come up with a nickname for Julius, who finally told the man, "If you want to call me something, call me the Doctor." It stuck.

At Roosevelt High, Julius starred in the classroom as well as on the basketball court. Unlike some of his friends from the playground, Julius never hung out on the streets at night, drinking or getting into trouble. Even on the playground basketball court, where arguments often broke out, Julius usually was able to avoid getting into fights.

By the time he was a senior, Julius was 6' 3" tall. Playing both guard and forward, he scored more than 20 points a game and helped Roosevelt to a 16–2 record.

Still, neither Julius nor the people around him realized just how good a player he was. Although many colleges showed interest in having him come play for them, he decided to attend the University of Massachusetts (UMass), a school that had never been known for its basketball team. The coach at UMass, Jack Leaman, was a friend of Julius's high school coach. Julius also didn't want to go too far from home because his brother was sick. Besides, Julius was hesitant to go to a school with a big basketball program because he believed that at those schools, you were not treated as an individual. He felt they took your body and used it.

As a sophomore at UMass, Julius averaged 25.7 points and 21 rebounds per game. The following summer, Coach Leaman helped Julius get a spot on the U.S. Olympic developmental team that played in Europe and the Soviet Union. Playing with the best college players from around the country, Julius found out that he was as good as any of them. In fact, he was the team's top scorer and rebounder.

CAREER HIGHLIGHTS: One of six players in NCAA history to average more than 20 points and 20 rebounds a game; one of only three players in NBA/ABA history to score 30,000 points; named MVP in American Basketball Association (1974, 1976) and the National Basketball Association (1981).

During his junior year at UMass, Julius averaged 26.9

points and 19.5 rebounds per game. The team had a 23–4 record, its best ever. And he did it all without the use of the shot that later became his trademark: the dunk. Dunking was not allowed in college basketball at the time.

In 1971, after his junior year, Julius decided to leave college to become a pro. He was one of only six players in NCAA Division I basketball history to average more than 20 points and 20 rebounds over the course of their college careers. He knew this would translate into real money in the pro ranks. His mother was upset with the decision but Julius knew his family could certainly use the money. He promised his mom that he would finish his course work and graduate from college one day — and he kept his promise. Fifteen years later, in 1986, Julius received his diploma from the University of Massachusetts!

> **WHEN** Scottie Pippen was 10 years old in 1975, Julius Erving was 25 and beginning his fifth and final season in the American Basketball Association. He led the New York Nets to the ABA title that season and was named the league's Most Valuable Player for the second time.

Julius had a chance to make a lot of money because the ABA, which had been organized four years earlier, was trying hard to become as big and as good as the older, better known NBA. Owners of some ABA teams were paying players big salaries to join their teams. Some of them were also signing players who had not yet completed their college careers in order to beat the NBA owners to the talent. This was because the NBA had a rule forbidding teams from signing players before their class graduated.

Julius hoped to play for the New York Nets, an ABA team

based on Long Island, but the Nets owner, Roy Boe, didn't approve of signing undergraduates. Earl Foreman, the owner of the Virginia Squires, didn't mind. He signed Julius to a four-year contract worth $500,000.

> **JULIUS SAID:** "My overall goal is to give people the feeling that they are being entertained by an artist — and to win."

Julius was an immediate star in the ABA, which encouraged showmanship with its red-white-and-blue ball and three-point baskets. (An NBA field goal at that time was worth just two points, no matter how long a shot it was.) Doctor J's colorful dunks and airborne antics became legendary. As a rookie, he scored 27.3 points a game during the regular season and averaged 33.3 points in the playoffs. In one game, he set an ABA playoff record with 53 points!

The next season, Julius led the league in scoring (31.9 points per game), but he wasn't happy playing in Virginia. He tried to jump to the NBA's Atlanta Hawks, but a court ordered him to return to the Squires. Then, in August 1973, Julius's dream came true: He became a member of the New York Nets. Mr. Boe, still the owner of the Nets, gave the Squires and the Hawks about $1 million and traded two players to Virginia for Doctor J. Mr. Boe then signed his new star to an eight-year contract worth about $2.5 million. The Doctor finally brought his show home to New York.

Julius led the Nets to ABA championships in 1974 and 1976, and he was named the league's Most Valuable Player in both seasons. He won three ABA scoring titles. At the 1976 All-Star Game, Doctor J won the first-ever Slam Dunk contest. Unfortunately, Julius's heroics were not as well known as they might have been because the ABA's games were not on television as often as NBA games.

In 1976, the ABA folded, and the Nets and three other ABA teams joined the NBA. Julius felt that, as the Nets' star attraction, he should be paid more and refused to play unless he was. The Nets management got angry and sold his contract to the Philadelphia 76ers, who gave Doctor J a new contract. Finally, the great Doctor J could show his stuff against all the best players in the country—and in front of millions of TV viewers.

OTHERS SAID: "The Doc changed basketball. He made the playground game official."
— Earvin "Magic" Johnson, former Los Angeles Lakers star.

It took Julius some time to feel comfortable in the new league. He wasn't the main man anymore because his team was full of other big stars. Slowly, though, Doctor J developed into the team's leader and the 76ers became a dominant force. He was named the Most Valuable Player in the league for the 1980–81 season, and he helped the 76ers win the NBA championship in 1983.

Doctor J spent 11 seasons with the 76ers. He was selected to play in the All-Star Game every year and was named MVP of that game twice. When he retired after the 1986–87 season, Julius had a career scoring average of 24.2 points per game and ranked among the 76ers all-time leaders in 15 categories. But he's remembered best for helping to bring a new style of play to professional basketball—an exciting, airborne, playground style that opened the door for high-fliers like Scottie Pippen.

And for this, basketball fans will forever be grateful.

CHAPTER TWO

BRETT HULL AND HIS HERO: ★ BOBBY HULL ★

It is not easy being the son or daughter of a famous athlete. It's especially hard if you decide to follow in the footsteps of your famous parent. It's harder still when the parent you are following is your own childhood hero.

Brett Hull, star goal scorer for the St. Louis Blues of the National Hockey League (NHL), learned this early on. Brett's boyhood hero was his father, Bobby Hull, one of the greatest goal scorers ever. Bobby, a left wing, scored more than 900 goals in a pro career that spanned 23 seasons. He was an outgoing person who always signed autographs — the fans loved him! What a hero he was to his young, shy, chubby son Brett.

Brett, a right wing, has his father's warm smile, but he is less outgoing and his playing style is different. In truth, Brett barely resembles his father on the ice — except when it comes to putting the puck in the net. Unlike Bobby, Brett is not a strong skater and he is not particularly good on defense. But Brett scores goals in huge numbers. In junior hockey, he once scored 105 goals in a single season! Since joining the NHL for good in 1987, he has led the league in goal-scoring with 70 or more goals three times.

"I have raised cattle, and I know a thing or two about genetics," said Bobby. "And I can tell you the biggest contribution I've made to Brett's success is providing him with the genes to do what he does well."

"Maybe I have his genes, but I definitely don't have his personality," said Brett. "I'm the laziest man alive. I'm not into expending physical energy. I'm into expending mental energy."

Bobby remembers the first time he saw his son play hockey. "It was in Winnipeg," Bobby told *The New York Times* in 1991. "He was perhaps seven, and he couldn't skate. The referee would pick him up and lug him to the other end of the ice

---

Brett learned to be his own person, despite following his famous father into pro hockey.

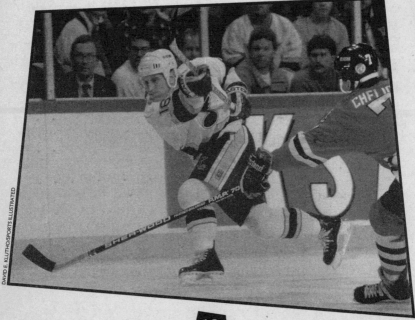

DAVID E. KLUTHO/SPORTS ILLUSTRATED

when the action moved. Then, he'd plop him down in front of the goal. Brett would never move. But he had the best action in his hands that I have ever seen.

"He never showed any enthusiasm. But the deal was, he was always there. Kids come up with excuses. Brett, whatever was going on in his mind, was always there. The kid who did the least work and scored the most goals."

BRETT SAYS: "I set a rule for myself: 'You will never be Bobby Hull. You will never, ever be as good as he was, so go out and play, and if you're pleased with your own effort, you have no worries in the world.' You see, I learned how to be Bobby Hull's kid a long, long time ago."

When Brett was 14 his parents divorced and he saw his father only occasionally for the next six years. The divorce hurt Brett deeply. He even considered quitting hockey, but he didn't. He went to the University of Minnesota at Duluth on a hockey scholarship. After two strong college seasons, Brett joined the Calgary Flames in 1986. He was sent to play on a minor-league team early the next season. Brett had a great year and played for Calgary the following season — until he was traded to the St. Louis Blues in March 1988.

In his first full season with the Blues, Brett scored 41 goals. The next season, 1989–90, Brett made the first of his three All-Star teams. In 1990–91, he was named the league's outstanding player by the players and MVP by the Professional Hockey Writers' Association. Brett and Bobby are the only father and son to both win NHL MVP awards.

Brett isn't just Bobby Hull's kid anymore. He is a hockey star in his own right.

★ BOBBY HULL ★

Some of the most effective players in hockey go almost unnoticed on the ice. It isn't until the game is over and you look at the statistics or listen to what the other players say that you realize what an impact one particular player had on a game.

But during his 23-year career in pro hockey, it was impossible not to notice Bobby Hull. He did everything with flair and flash. More than any other player, Bobby was responsible for the growth of hockey's popularity in the United States during the 1960's and early 1970's. And he turned the Chicago Blackhawks of the National Hockey League from a financial flop into a box office gold mine almost single-handedly.

Bobby was nicknamed "Golden Jet." He was physically strong, incredibly fast, and the owner of the hardest shot in the NHL. His slapshot was clocked at 118.3 miles per hour! He electrified the fans with mad dashes down the ice, his blond hair whipping back because players were not yet required to wear helmets. The sight of Bobby streaking down the ice at 28.3 miles per hour with his curved stick cradling the puck brought fear to the faces of many goaltenders. Remember, back in Bobby's prime years, most goalies didn't wear masks to protect their faces!

Despite being hounded by opposing players who tried to knock him out of action, Bobby led the NHL in goals scored seven times. In Bobby's day, scoring 50 goals in a season was like hitting 60 home runs — hardly anyone ever did it. But he reached the 50-goal mark nine times. No one else had ever done it more than once!

Bobby scored 610 goals in 16 NHL seasons. He also left the NHL in 1972 for a period of seven years to join a new league, the World Hockey Association. In seven WHA seasons, with the Winnipeg Jets, Bobby scored another 303 goals, including a career-high 77 in 1974–75.

Not bad for a kid from a town so small that the dogs were thought to outnumber the people! "The population is about a thousand people, if you count the dogs," Bobby's sister, Judy,

---

Bobby was called the "Golden Jet" because of his blond hair and the way he flew down the ice.

AP / WIDE WORLD PHOTOS

once told *Sports Illustrated*. "About a hundred if you don't."
She may have been kidding, but Point Anne, Ontario, Canada,
was not a big city.

Name: Robert Marvin Hull
Nicknames: Bobby, "Golden Jet"
Born: January 3, 1939, Point
Anne, Ontario, Canada
Height: 5' 10" **Weight:** 193 lbs.
Cool fact: Bobby was one of the
first to popularize the curved
hockey stick. He used to bend
the blades around door jams The
curved stick creates a greater
whipping action and delivers
harder shots and passes.

Robert Marvin Hull
was born there on January
3, 1939, the eldest boy and
fifth of 11 children. His
father was a foreman at a
cement company, and
Bobby grew up in a series
of houses owned by the
company in different
locations around town.
He learned to skate and
play hockey on the ice of
the Bay of Quinte, just outside one of those homes. It was
clear early on that he was a natural athlete.

"We gave Robert a pair of skates for Christmas when he
wasn't quite three," his father, Robert Edward Hull, told *Sports
Illustrated*. "I took him over to a frozen pond near home, and
I'll be darned if he wasn't taking a few strides within a half
hour.

"He learned to swim just as fast. One day he just waded
out into the water and started paddling away. Begad, I had to
wade in after him, clothes and all!"

Bobby's dad had been a good amateur hockey player as a
young man and he encouraged Bobby to play as much as he
could. Bobby didn't need much encouragement! Like many
kids in Canada, he played hockey almost around the clock,
both at home and at school.

"I'd wake up early, build the fire in the kitchen and go out to the rink to bang pucks off the boards for hours," Bobby told *The New York Times* in 1991. "The neighbors used to beg my father to make me wait at least until 7 a.m. before doing it.

"As a kid I never walked from here to there, I didn't trot from here to there. I ran. And I couldn't wait for winter. My father would sometimes find me in the heat of summer standing in the house with all my hockey equipment on, sweating crazily. I just wanted the feel of it. Hockey had become an obsession."

When Bobby was 14, a scout for the Chicago Blackhawks named Bob Wilson spotted him and signed him up with the Chicago organization. (Back then, there was no formal NHL draft. The clubs signed up potential stars whenever they could and had arrangements with amateur teams to help develop their young talent.) Bobby was sent 173 miles away from home to play for a Junior B team. He would cry nights and look forward to the weekends when his parents would be able to visit him.

CAREER HIGHLIGHTS: One of only two players to be named MVP in both the NHL and the WHA, which he did twice in each league; led the NHL in goals scored 7 times and WHA once; scored 77 goals in 1974–75 season for Winnipeg of WHA, the most ever scored in a single season in that league.

"You have to bear burdens like that," Bobby said. "It's part of growing up in Canada if you want to make the NHL."

Bobby moved up to Junior A hockey, but it took him a while to develop the talent that eventually made him a star. In the juniors, he was mostly known as a hard-skating center with no great reputation for reliability or teamwork. In fact, on at least one occasion, Bobby was suspended from the team for his lack of teamwork.

"I reprimanded Bobby just as some father would reprimand his own son for tromping on the living room rug with his muddy shoes," said Rudy Pilous, one of Bobby's amateur coaches and later his coach with the Blackhawks. "We were trying to get him to move the puck, to help set up plays, but he was headstrong and couldn't see things our way."

At 18, Bobby made the big jump from the amateur ranks to the NHL. He was still inexperienced and far from mature, but the crowds loved his style and good nature. Bobby also was very generous with his time off the ice, always stopping to sign autographs for fans outside the arena. "I've never seen him turn his back on a kid," said his teammate Tony Esposito, a goaltender. "He considers autograph-signing an obligation."

WHEN Brett Hull was 10 years old in 1974, Bobby Hull was 35 and beginning his third season in the World Hockey Association with the Winnipeg Jets. He scored a league-leading 77 goals that season and won the league's Most Valuable Player award.

But Bobby didn't really come of age as a hockey player until 1959, when he went on an off-season exhibition tour of Europe. His team was scheduled to play 23 games in 25 nights, but Bobby was determined to see all the sights of Europe along the way. His daily excursions tired him out so that he did not have the energy at night to take the puck from end to end as he usually did. He had to pass the puck off and, in so doing, he learned the value of team play.

Bobby became a full-fledged star the next season, his third. He led the NHL in scoring with 39 goals and 42 assists. In his fourth season, 1960–61, Bobby teamed with center Stan Mikita to bring the Blackhawks their first Stanley Cup championship in 23 years! Although Bobby and Stan didn't bring any more championships to Chicago, they were powerful forces in hockey during the 1960's. Between them, they

BOBBY SAID: "Setting an example for kids should be hockey's main theme. Body checking and aggressiveness are part of hockey. So is the odd fight, because of the tempo. But not the intimidation, the stick-swinging, the high stick, the spear. That's not hockey."

won four MVP awards and led the league in scoring six times! In 1965–66, Bobby set an NHL single-season record for scoring, with 54 goals and 97 points. No player had ever scored more than 50 goals in a season before!

Part of Bobby's success came from the fact that he was one of the pioneers of the curved stick. The curved blade gave his shots more speed, power, and lift than anyone was used to. It was no accident that goalies started wearing facemasks during Bobby's era!

Bobby played with the Blackhawks through the 1971–72 season, but he became unhappy with the people who managed the team. In 1972, he did the unthinkable: He jumped to another league! Bobby joined the World Hockey Association, which had just been formed. The WHA owners knew that having a big-name player like Bobby would do wonders for their league. He was given a startling $2.75 million for 10 seasons to join the Winnipeg Jets and put the WHA on the map.

And Bobby did just that. The uproar over his move was incredible. The NHL was so upset that it sued to try to keep Bobby and other NHL players from joining the upstart WHA. Although Bobby missed a few games because of that lawsuit, he scored 51 goals and 52 assists in 63 games and was named the WHA's Most Valuable Player. He earned that honor again for the 1974–75 season, when he scored 142 points, an amazing total for a left winger.

> **OTHERS SAID:** "To say that Bobby was a great hockey player is to labor the point. He was all of that, of course. But the thing I admired about him was the way he handled people. He always enjoyed signing autographs for the fans and was a genuine nice guy." — *Stan Mikita, the Blackhawks' Hall of Fame center and teammate of Bobby's.*

With the Jets, Bobby, now in his late 30s, played on a line with two great, young players from Sweden, Ulf Nilsson and Anders Hedberg. "They make the game fun for me," Bobby said at the time. "They're also my legs." Bobby, Ulf, and Anders led Winnipeg to the WHA Championship in 1976 and again in 1978.

Bobby slowed down after that. He was 39 years old and shoulder injuries forced him to the sidelines repeatedly. He played just four games in 1978–79 and, in February 1980, the Jets traded Bobby to the Hartford Whalers. By that time, the WHA and NHL had merged. NHL fans were looking forward to seeing Bobby again, but he was able to play only 27 games. Bobby hung up his skates for good after the 1979–80 season. He was 41. The Golden Jet had finally landed.

Bobby was elected to the Hockey Hall of Fame in 1983. Maybe his son Brett will join him there someday.

CHAPTER THREE

BARRY SANDERS AND HIS HERO: ★ MUHAMMAD ALI ★

Barry Sanders is one of the smallest players in the National Football League (NFL), but the Detroit Lions' star running back puts up some of the biggest numbers. And for a small guy, he's known to have a big, and generous, heart.

Barry stands only 5' 8" tall and weighs 203 pounds. But he is strong, fast, and tough to tackle. He can run the 40-yard dash in 4.27 seconds and can squat-lift 557 pounds. He can jump 41½ inches high from a standing start. Those qualities helped him win the 1988 Heisman Trophy as the best college football player in the country. They also helped him become one of the best offensive players in the NFL.

But none of this was easy for Barry. When he was growing up, few people believed he could be a great football player. So Barry sat on the bench, played a little defense, and was patient.

He first played football in his neighborhood in Wichita, Kansas. Sometimes as many as 20 kids were on a side and most of them were bigger than Barry. "From fourth grade on, I was always smaller than most kids," Barry told *Sports Illustrated For Kids* magazine. "It was intimidating, but I liked the game and I wanted to play." So Barry learned how to avoid tacklers — still one of his greatest talents. He's sometimes scared by the NFL's 270-pound tacklers. But he welcomes the challenge. "I think every good runner runs scared," he said. "It's the fear that comes from not wanting to get caught, like when you're playing tag and you don't want whoever is 'it' to get you."

Off the field, Barry is shy and quiet. When he won the Heisman, he almost didn't participate in the award ceremony. "I have a problem being put on a pedestal just because I run fast," Barry said. "There's a lot more to a person than that."

Barry never let his small size get in the way of his dream of making it big in the NFL.

AL TIELEMANS/SPORTS ILLUSTRATED

There's certainly more to Barry. He's a very caring person who gives money generously to his family's church in Wichita and to other charities every year. Once he heard that a Wichita supermarket was going out of business and that many elderly and poor people would have no place nearby to buy food. Barry bought the supermarket and gave it to his family to run. "I want to make a difference in people's lives," Barry said. "I'm not the type of person who sits around and wonders about what makes me so good."

> **BARRY SAYS:** "I never met Ali, but I'd sure like to. I think I'd let him do the talking, though."

Barry's parents, William and Shirley Sanders, tried to instill strong values in all 11 of their children. They taught them that if you work hard and never give up, good things can happen to you. "Seeing my mom and dad raise 11 kids against the odds they faced gave me confidence in what I could do," Barry said.

Besides his family, the one person who inspired Barry during his youth was boxer Muhammad Ali. Ali was one of the greatest heavyweight champions in history, but he also was an outspoken critic of racial injustice. He was an extremely confident — and talkative — athlete.

"All of my friends admired him, too," says Barry. "He was so good at what he did. I used to catch his fights on TV with my brother and father."

Barry wanted to be good at what he did, too, but he had trouble just getting a chance to play. When he was in 10th grade at Wichita's North High School, he was on the junior varsity team, but saw very little action. Even though Barry was a good runner, the coach thought he was too small.

Barry made the varsity in 11th grade, joining his brother Byron on the team. Byron was a tailback and a good one, so rather than compete against his brother, Barry played cornerback and receiver. After Byron graduated, Barry moved to running back. It wasn't until the fourth game of his senior year that Barry became the starting tailback. He gained 274 yards that day and went on to gain 1,417 yards for the season!

Still, only two colleges offered Barry scholarships because he was so small. He chose Oklahoma State University, and spent the first two years there as a backup. Instead of moping, though, Barry practiced hard, built up his body, and made the most of the playing time he did get. In Oklahoma State's first game of the 1987 season, Barry returned the opening kickoff 100 yards for a touchdown. He did the same thing in the first game of the 1988 season!

As a junior, Barry finally became a star. He set 13 NCAA Division I-A records, including most rushing yards (2,628), touchdowns (39), and points scored (234). He won the Heisman Trophy. When Oklahoma State was placed on probation by the NCAA for recruiting violations the next spring, Barry decided to pass up his senior year and turn pro. The Lions made him the third pick in the 1989 NFL draft.

Since then, Barry has become one of the NFL's best running backs. He led the league in rushing in 1990, became only the fourth player to rush for more than 1,000 yards in his first four seasons, and has broken or tied 11 Detroit offensive records.

Like his hero, Muhammad Ali, Barry Sanders is a tough guy to bring down.

★ MUHAMMAD ALI ★

Muhammad Ali may have been the best-known athlete in history. He was certainly one of the most controversial.

Ali, as he was often called, even by friends, was the only boxer to win the world heavyweight championship three times. He earned more than $60 million in prize money during his career. He was very strong and very quick, a combination that sets him apart from most heavyweights, even other champions. "Float like a butterfly, sting like a bee" was the

Ali was a champion who always stuck by his beliefs, even when they were unpopular.

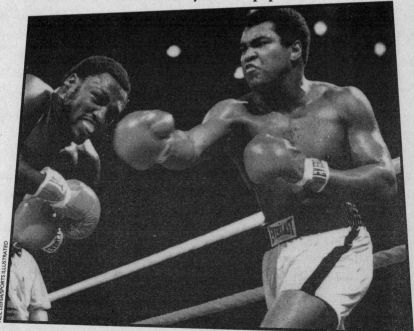

NEIL LEIFER/SPORTS ILLUSTRATED

advice he was once given by one of his assistant trainers, Drew "Bundini" Brown. That advice served him well.

Being a boxing superstar made up only one part of this amazing man's life. Quick-witted, sharp-tongued, cocky, and proud are only some of the adjectives used to describe Ali. He was a poet, a religion teacher, and an anti-war activist. He was known all over the world and drew large crowds wherever he went. And, perhaps most of all, Ali was a symbol for black people everywhere. He fought harder out of the ring than in it to preserve the pride of African-Americans.

"I am the greatest," Ali used to tell the world. Whether or not he was the greatest heavyweight champ ever, in terms of personality and purpose, he was unlike any other.

It all began in the city of Louisville, Kentucky, where Ali was born Cassius Marcellus Clay, Junior, on January 17, 1942. His father was a sign painter and his mother did housework for other families. Young Cassius's great uncle had been a slave owned by Cassius [*cash-yus*] Marcellus Clay of Kentucky, who was the American ambassador to Russia in the 1860's. After being freed, the uncle took the name of his former master, and the name was then passed down the generations.

Cassius first became interested in boxing at the age of 12.

Name: Muhammad Ali (born Cassius Marcellus Clay, Junior)
Nicknames: "The Greatest," "The Louisville Lip."
Born: January 17, 1942, Louisville, Kentucky
Height: 6' 3"   **Weight:** 230 lbs.
Cool Fact: Ali once fought a Japanese wrestler named Antonio Inoki to prove that a boxer could defeat a wrestler. The match was declared a draw after 15 boring rounds.

He was attending a fair in downtown Louisville and someone stole his new bike. Cassius went to a policeman to complain. In tears, he told the policeman he was "gonna whip [the thief] if I can find him." The policeman, Joe Martin, asked Cassius if he could fight. "You better learn to fight before you start fighting," Officer Martin said. Officer Martin was training an amateur boxing team and he got Cassius interested.

Although he weighed only 89 pounds, Cassius was confident right from the start. In his first six years in the sport, Cassius fought 108 amateur bouts, winning 100 of them.

CAREER HIGHLIGHTS: Won Olympic gold medal as light heavyweight in 1960; only heavyweight to win title three times; earned more than $60 million as a professional fighter.

"His secret was his unusual eye speed," said Officer Martin. "It was blinding."

Cassius became a national celebrity in the summer of 1960, when he won the gold medal in the light heavyweight division at the Olympics. He returned home to a hero's welcome and decided to turn pro. Cassius won his first professional fight on October 29, 1960, over veteran boxer Tunney Hunsaker, who was out of shape. By the end of his second professional season, Cassius had won 16 fights in a row.

Cassius was becoming well known for telling everyone how great he was, often in rhyme. He also started predicting the round in which he would knock out his opponent. All this talk earned him the nicknames, "The Louisville Lip," "Mighty Mouth," and "Cassius the Brashest." The self-promotion worked, however. Fans started to watch him fight.

In February 1964, Cassius got the chance to fight Sonny

Liston for the heavyweight title. Sonny was a devastating puncher and not many thought Cassius had a chance against the veteran. But it was clear from the opening bell that Cassius had better speed. Sonny's punches didn't connect and Cassius's did. When Sonny failed to answer the bell for the seventh round, Cassius was the new champion.

"Eat your words," he screamed at the press before leaving the ring. "I am the greatest! I — am — the — greatest!"

> **WHEN** Barry Sanders was 10 years old in 1978, Muhammad Ali was 36 and nearing the end of his brilliant boxing career. He lost to Leon Spinks in a stunning upset in February, but beat Leon seven months later to become the only heavyweight champion in history to regain the title three times.

He might have been the most popular champion ever, but he did two things that many people didn't like: He joined the Black Muslims and he refused to serve in the Army during the Vietnam War. Both were controversial actions that made him many enemies and disappointed many fans, but they were actions that Ali believed in, and he stuck by his beliefs.

After winning his first heavyweight title in 1964, Ali announced he had joined the Black Muslim religion. The Black Muslims combined aspects of the Islamic religion with some of their own beliefs. They worshipped Allah, had strict rules about diet and behavior, and believed blacks and whites should live apart. Ali now said that Cassius Clay was his "slave name." "From now on, I'm Muhammad Ali," he said.

The black world applauded its new hero, but much of white America was confused and angry. His religious conversion was nothing, however, compared to the bombshell he dropped on the public in 1967. He had successfully defended his title nine times and had grown in popularity. Meanwhile, the war in Vietnam was getting more intense and soldiers were needed. Ali was eligible to be drafted into the Army, but he asked to be excused on the grounds that he was a Muslim minister. His request was turned down.

On April 28, 1967, Ali was called to join the Army, but he refused. On June 25, 1967, Ali was convicted of evading the draft, sentenced to five years in prison, and fined $10,000. The New York State Athletic Commission stripped him of his boxing license and his heavyweight title. The World Boxing Association took away its title, too.

Ali was released from prison while his lawyers appealed his conviction. They took the case all the way to the U.S. Supreme Court and, in June 1971, the highest court in the country overturned his conviction. The Court ruled, 8–0, that the draft board had been wrong to deny Ali's claim that he shouldn't have to serve in the military because it conflicted with his religion.

ALI SAID: "My life has been a lot of fun, a lot of suffering and a lot of pain. It has also been a lot of testing: being black in America and saying the things you want to say and exercise real freedom. My life has made me controversial; it has made me different."

Meanwhile, the boxing commissions and promoters turned their backs on him after the conviction. A new champion was named. While he couldn't box, Ali made speeches at colleges and Muslim meetings. He was in much demand as a speaker.

On October 26, 1970, Ali's unofficial banishment from boxing came to an end. He returned to the ring with a three-round technical knockout of Jerry Quarry in Atlanta, Georgia. On December 7, he knocked out Oscar Bonavena of Argentina in the 15th round of their fight. That set the stage for a showdown between Ali and Joe Frazier, who had won the unified heavyweight title while Ali was still banished in 1970.

The fight between Ali and Joe was scheduled for March 8, 1971, and each fighter was guaranteed $2.5 million. The fight went the distance (the full number of rounds) and Joe was awarded a unanimous decision. It was Ali's first loss in 32 bouts.

> **OTHERS SAID:** "This man drew people like he was God himself. Once, in Korea, we couldn't move from the plane to the terminal because of the crowd. And, as normal as it was for black people to love him, he represented something that all people, black and white, could look up to." — *Murad Muhammad, a former bodyguard of Ali's.*

Ali fought 13 times in the next three years and earned $3.8 million. He lost one bout, to a young fighter named Ken Norton, whom he then beat in a rematch. He also got to fight Joe Frazier again — and this time, in 1974, he beat him. But the heavyweight title was not at stake; Joe had lost it to a former Olympic champion named George Foreman.

Ali finally got a chance to fight George for the title in 1974, in Kinshasa, the capital of the African republic of Zaire. "A rumble in the jungle," Ali called it. Ali knocked out George in the eighth round. At last, Ali was champion again!

Every heavyweight wanted to fight the champ, including

Joe Frazier. In September 1975, Ali fought Joe a third time. The bout was held in Manila, the capital of the Philippines and advertised as "The Thrilla in Manila." In a brutal slugging match watched by millions of people worldwide on closed circuit TV, Ali emerged as the winner again.

Ali suffered one of the most embarassing losses of his career three years later. He was beaten by a 25-year-old named Leon Spinks in February 1978. Leon was 12 years younger than Ali, and the bout was awarded to him on a split decision, which means that the judges didn't all agree on who had won. Still, it was one of the most stunning upsets in boxing history. It didn't take long, though, for Ali to get his revenge. In September, he regained the title for a record third time by defeating Leon.

Soon after that, Ali announced his retirement from boxing. He couldn't stay away from the ring, though, but he should have. He returned in 1980 to face Larry Holmes, the tough, undefeated champion, but he lost in 11 rounds. Ali fought once more, losing to Trevor Berbick, a fighter he would easily have beaten in his prime. Then he retired for good.

Ali continued to tour around the world. In 1984, he was diagnosed as having Parkinson's syndrome, a nerve disorder. His speech had become slurred and he had trouble moving around. The old Ali who floated like a butterfly and stung like a bee was no more. Too many punches to the head during his long career may have taken their toll.

Still, no matter where he went, his mere presence brought cries of "Ali, Ali" from the crowds. No athlete ever received so much respect from so many.

CHAPTER FOUR

JACKIE JOYNER-KERSEE AND HER HERO: ★ BABE DIDRIKSON ★

When Jackie Joyner-Kersee was born in 1962, her great-grandmother, Ollie Mae Johnson, named her Jacqueline after President John F. Kennedy's wife, Jacqueline. "Someday, this little girl is going to be the First Lady of something," said Mrs. Johnson. She was right. Jackie grew up to be the First Lady of track and field.

Many sports fans think that Jackie is more than just a track and field athlete. They say that she is the world's best female athlete! Jackie competes in the heptathlon, a grueling two-day, seven-event contest. (*Hepta* is the Greek word for seven.) The seven events are the 100-meter hurdles, the shot put, high jump, 200-meter run, long jump, javelin, and 800-meter run. Competitors earn points based on the times of their runs, the distances of their throws, and the lengths or heights of their jumps. The person with the most points at the end of the second day is the winner. The heptathlon was created in 1981 from the pentathlon, which had five events (*penta* means five). Women competed in the pentathlon from 1950 until 1981 in the United States.

Jackie has set the standard in the heptathlon. She won gold

ANDY HAYT / SPORTS ILLUSTRATED

Because she's so good at so many events, Jackie has been called the best female athlete in the world today.

medals in the event at both the 1988 and 1992 Summer Olympics and at the 1987 and 1993 world championships. Her best score of 7,291 points is more than 200 points better than anyone else's — and a world record.

In addition, Jackie is one of the world's top long jumpers. She won a gold medal in that event at the 1987 and 1991 world championships and at the 1988 Olympics. She has also set American records in the hurdles.

Jackie has excelled in sports since she was a child growing up in East St. Louis, Illinois. She lived with her parents, her brother, Al (who grew up to become an Olympic champion in the triple jump), and two younger sisters, Angela and Debra, in a very poor section of the city. The Joyners did not have much money, and there wasn't always enough to eat. But they had a loving home. Mr. and Mrs. Joyner made sure that their children learned right from wrong and that they worked hard in school.

One day Jackie saw a television program about Babe Didrikson Zaharias, a famous athlete who competed in track and field in the 1930's and in golf in the 1930's through 1950's. Babe had died of cancer six years before Jackie was born, but her legend was inspiring.

> **JACKIE SAYS:** "As a woman, Babe was a great role model. She made me believe that girls could do great things in sports."

"I learned her story from something I saw on TV and I thought, 'Wow! That's incredible!'" said Jackie. "I was so impressed with her ability. She was good at so many things: track, basketball, golf, you name it. What Babe accomplished was amazing, especially when you consider the conditions in which she competed!

"I was also interested in her because she was a multi-event track athlete," said Jackie. "There was no heptathlon then but she showed me that you could be good in a lot of different events.

Using Babe as her inspiration, Jackie became more and more involved with sports. She was a star on the girls' basketball team at Lincoln High School, averaging 19.6 points per game as a senior forward. She was captain of the volleyball team, led her track team to three state titles, and set the state record in the long jump. She also graduated near the top of her class.

Jackie's combination of good grades and athletic skills earned her a basketball scholarship to the University of California at Los Angeles (UCLA). She started at forward for four years and competed for the track team. Jackie was named Most Valuable Player in both of those sports!

While in college, Jackie learned that she had asthma, an illness in which the bronchial tubes in the throat swell up, making it difficult for a person to breathe. It can be caused by many things, but in Jackie's case, it was believed to be brought on by exercise. But that didn't slow her down. She learned to manage her condition so that she could still compete.

After graduating from college, Jackie concentrated on track and field. Her coach and husband, Bob Kersee, helped her become the best in the world. A practical joker and chatterbox away from the athletic field, Jackie is all business when she is competing. She works out five days a week and each workout is at least five hours long.

Jackie's busy competition schedule takes her to all parts of the world, but she still finds time to help kids. She formed the Jackie Joyner-Kersee Community Foundation to help children in her hometown and she speaks to groups of kids at schools and clubs around the country. When she speaks to kids, Jackie tells them: "It's important to understand who you are and what it is that you want to do. Don't be afraid to be different."

That is a lesson that Jackie probably picked up from her hero, because Babe Didrikson Zaharias was definitely one of a kind!

★ BABE DIDRIKSON ZAHARIAS ★

Name a sport. Any sport. Chances are Babe Didrikson Zaharias could play it, and play it very well.

Babe was only 5' 7" and she weighed just 130 pounds. But she could do it all: She averaged more than 30 points per game as a top-notch amateur basketball player. She was an Olympic champion in track and field. She dominated the women's professional golf tour in the late 1940's and early 1950's. But that's not all. Babe was also great at baseball, bowling, skating, billiards, polo, and tennis. She could punt a football long distances. She even pitched for major league baseball teams in exhibition games!

Babe was named Woman Athlete of the Year by the Associated Press six times and in 1950, the same organization voted her Woman Athlete of the First Half of the 20th Century. Today, more than 40 years later, she is still remembered as one of the most amazing athletes in American history.

There wasn't much that was amazing about Babe's beginnings, however. Born Mildred Ella Didrikson in 1914 in Port Arthur, Texas, she was the sixth of seven children. Her parents had moved to Texas from Norway

Name: Mildred Ella Didrikson Zaharias
Nickname: Babe
Height: 5' 7"   **Weight:** 130 lbs.
Born: June 26, 1914, Port Arthur, Texas
Died: September 27, 1956, Galveston, Texas
Cool fact: Babe had a real sweet tooth. Her first track coach once offered to buy her a chocolate soda if she cleared 5' 3" in the high jump, then a world record for women. Babe earned her soda in practice!

At the 1932 Olympics, Babe won three medals, including a gold in the javelin.

after Mr. Didrikson's career as a ship's carpenter was over. Babe's mother had enjoyed skiing and skating in Norway but, by the time Babe was born, Mrs. Didrikson was busy raising her growing family.

The Didriksons moved to Beaumont, Texas, when Mildred was 3. Mr. Didrikson built his kids a backyard gymnasium with weight equipment and chinning bars. Mildred enjoyed the jungle gym, along with her brothers and sisters.

At about the age of 7, Mildred earned her nickname when she hit five home runs in a baseball game she was playing with a group of boys. The kids began calling her "Babe" after great New York Yankees' slugger Babe Ruth. People rarely called her Mildred again.

By about the age of 8, Babe was much better than most boys at baseball and football. She was even great at marbles. In fact, she was good at just about everything she tried. No one in Beaumont had ever seen anything quite like it.

Some people didn't know what to make of Babe. At the time, women's sports weren't taken seriously and people often looked down on girls who played sports. They thought girls should look and act a certain way, and it definitely wasn't the way that Babe looked and acted. She wore boyish clothes and played the harmonica, which back then was considered an instrument for boys only.

CAREER HIGHLIGHTS: Won gold medals in 80-meter hurdles and javelin and silver medal in high jump in 1932 Summer Olympics; won 82 golf tournaments, including 17 in a row; was named Woman Athlete of the Year six times and was named Woman Athlete of the First Half of the 20th Century by Associated Press.

Being different made it hard for Babe at school. She was teased often. But that didn't bother her because she enjoyed competing so much.

"Before I was even in my teens," she wrote in her autobiography, *This Life I've Led,* "I knew exactly what I wanted to be when I grew up: The greatest athlete that ever lived."

Babe got her start in that direction when she was 16. She was playing girls' basketball at Beaumont High School when she was spotted by Colonel Melvin J. McCombs, who coached a basketball team for an insurance company in Dallas. Colonel McCombs took Babe, who hadn't graduated from high school, to Dallas to learn to be a stenographer, a kind of secretary — and to play for the company basketball team. It wasn't long before Babe's team, the Golden Cyclones, was one of the best in the league.

In 1930, Colonel McCombs organized a track team. Babe competed in every event. In her very first track meet, she won four gold medals! Over the next two years, she established herself as the best female track and field athlete in the country. Babe decided to try out for the Olympics in 1932.

In July 1932, track teams from all over the country gathered in Evanston, Illinois, which would also serve as tryouts for the U.S. Olympic team. Most of the teams had several athletes trying for spots on the U.S. team but the Golden Cyclones of Dallas, Texas, had just one: Babe. But that was enough. Babe scored in seven of the eight events she entered and won the national team title all by herself! She won five events, setting world records in four, and tied for first in another.

WHEN Jackie Joyner-Kersee was 10 years old in 1972, Babe Didrikson Zaharias had been dead for 16 years. However, Jackie was inspired by Babe after seeing a movie on her athletic exploits. If Babe had lived, she would have been 74 when Jackie won two gold medals at the 1988 Summer Olympics in Seoul, South Korea.

Under the rules at the time, however, Olympic competitors were not allowed to participate in more than three events, so Babe chose to compete in the javelin, the 80-meter hurdles, and the high jump at the Olympics, which were to start in Los

45

Angeles later in the month of July.

Even against the best athletes in the world, Babe stood out.

> **BABE SAID:** "I never just wished for something. I always went to work to get it."

She won the javelin and the 80-meter hurdles and placed second in the high jump. In that event, she and U.S. teammate Jean Shiley both cleared 5' 5¼", then a world-record height. Jean was awarded the gold medal, however, because the judges ruled that Babe's head had crossed over the bar before her feet, which was not allowed at the time.

After the Olympics, Babe was suspended by the Amateur Athletic Union when her picture appeared in an advertisement. Amateur athletes were not allowed to profit from their fame as athletes. So, to earn money, she went on stage and performed all kinds of athletic feats. She would run on a treadmill to show off her running form or shoot plastic golf balls into the audience. She toured the country giving billiards exhibitions. Babe also traveled around the country with her own basketball team. She often played in small towns against any team, male or female, that would challenge her. She earned more than $40,000 in her first three years of doing these entertaining exhibitions.

But Babe missed the thrill of competing against the best athletes in the world. And she wanted a sport that would give her recognition. She decided that professional golf was the ticket. So, at the age of 20, Babe took up yet

> **OTHERS SAID:** "She is without any question the athletic phenomenon of all time, man or woman," sportswriter Grantland Rice wrote of Babe.

another sport in order to get back into competition.

Most sports came easily to Babe. Golf did not. But she was determined to master it. In 1933 she would get to the golf course each weekday at 5:00 in the morning to practice. On weekends, she practiced golf 16 hours a day! "I'd hit golf balls until my hands were bloody and sore," she said. By 1935, she was the Texas state champion. From 1940 to 1950, Babe dominated women's golf. She won every major tournament at least once. She was the first American to win the British Amateur. At one point, she won 17 tournaments in a row — a feat that almost certainly won't be matched. Babe competed as an amateur until 1947, and then was one of the founders of the Ladies Professional Golf Association. She tore up the professional golf tour from 1948 to 1955, winning 31 events.

> **BABE SAID:** "Is there anything you don't play?" sportswriter Paul Gallico of the *New York Daily News* once asked Babe. "Yeah," she said. "Dolls."

She met her future husband, professional wrestler George Zaharias, at a golf tournament. They married in 1938.

In 1953, Babe was diagnosed with cancer and had major surgery. She was told that she would never play golf again. But Babe was a competitor — even against cancer. Not only did she continue to play golf in 1954 and 1955, but she won seven tournaments, including the important 1954 U.S. Women's Open championship.

Babe died of cancer in 1956, at age 42. But her legend lives on and serves as an inspiration for others. Just ask Jackie Joyner-Kersee!

CHAPTER FIVE

CAL RIPKEN, JUNIOR AND HIS HERO: ★ BROOKS ROBINSON ★

Cal Ripken, Junior, practically grew up on a baseball field. His father, Cal Ripken, Senior, was a player, coach, and minor league manager in the Baltimore Orioles organization for many years. He would often take two of his sons, Cal and Billy, with him to practices and games. Cal and his brother learned a lot about baseball just from watching the pros. Cal senior didn't push his sons into baseball, though. In fact, his other son, Fred, gave up baseball when he was 9 years old because he didn't want to practice.

Cal senior talked baseball to his kids a lot. They would discuss baseball at the dinner table and on long car rides. Cal senior even told little Cal baseball bedtime stories.

"He would tell me stories about foul tips splintering up his fingers and how he'd have to tape them together so he could play," said Cal junior.

Although the family lived in Aberdeen, Maryland, each summer they would pack up the car and travel to wherever Cal senior was working. Since Cal senior moved around from team to team, the Ripkens spent summers in many different parts of the United States. Cal senior kept playing until 1964, when he

Cal, a two-time American League MVP, grew up listening to baseball bedtime stories.

RONALD C. MODRA/SPORTS ILLUSTRATED

turned to managing in the minor leagues. He then was scouting and eventually started coaching in 1976.

Cal junior played Little League and Babe Ruth League baseball. In high school, he was a star pitcher and a shortstop. He was selected in the second round of the 1978 draft and four years later was the American League's Rookie of the Year.

Over the years, Cal junior got to know all of the Orioles players. The one he admired most was Brooks Robinson, the team's All-Star third baseman.

"Like thousands of kids who grew up in Baltimore in the 1960's, I had Brooks Robinson as my hero," says Cal. "He was the guy who best represented what those great Oriole teams were all about. He was a clutch hitter who came through with the big hit when the team needed it. And he made so many great defensive plays!"

Cal junior grew up to be a lot like his hero. Brooks was one of the best fielders in history, a good hitter who had decent power, and a player who could be counted on to be in the lineup almost every day.

Cal was twice named the American League Most Valuable Player, and helped the Orioles get to the 1983 World Series, in which they beat the Philadelphia Phillies. At 6' 4" and 220 pounds, Cal is the tallest shortstop ever to play regularly in the major leagues. But that hasn't stopped him from becoming a standout defensive player, like Brooks. He has won two Gold Glove Awards.

> **CAL SAYS:** "Naturally, with my dad working in the Oriole organization, I had the chance to meet Brooks Robinson. And I found out he was just as great a person off the field as he was on it."

Cal is also a steady performer on offense. From 1982 through 1991, he hit 20 or more homers a season, a record for shortstops. Cal has also driven in 72 or more runs in each of 12 straight seasons.

And as far as being in the lineup is concerned, through the 1993 season, Cal had played 1,897 consecutive games — second only to Lou Gehrig's 2,130.

Off the field, Cal junior has taken after his boyhood hero by giving of his time to others. In 1992, he won the Roberto Clemente Award as the major league player who gave the most to his team and the community. Brooks Robinson won that award in 1972.

★ BROOKS ROBINSON ★

Brooks Robinson was not a fast runner. He did not have a very strong throwing arm, either. He had average power and a fairly ordinary batting average. Yet he was one of the best third basemen ever to play in the major leagues.

What made him so great? He had wonderful hands and reflexes that enabled him to field his position better than anyone else. His reflexes were so quick that opponents called him "the vacuum cleaner" for scooping up everything hit his way.

**Brooks combined great skill at third base
with an ability to get clutch hits.**

HERB SCHARFMAN/SPORTS ILLUSTRATED

While he didn't get a lot of hits or homers, he got them when it really counted. That's why he is considered one of the best "clutch hitters" of all time. Brooks hit well when there were runners on base in scoring position. His lifetime batting average was only .267, but he drove in 75 or more runs in a season 10 times!

Brooks played 23 seasons in the major leagues, all of them with the Baltimore Orioles. He played in five American League Championship Series (ALCS) and in four World Series. He also led the league in fielding percentage 11 times and in assists 8 times. (A player gets an assist when he throws out an opposing runner.)

Name: Brooks Calbert Robinson, Junior
Nickname: Brooksie
Born: May 18, 1937, Little Rock, Arkansas
Height: 6' 1" **Weight:** 180 lbs.
COOL FACT: As a rookie, Brooks was instructed by veteran infielder George Kell. George had been one of the best third basemen in the A.L. during the 1940's and 1950's and played just two seasons with the Orioles. In 1983, Brooks and George were inducted into the Baseball Hall of Fame at the same time!

Playing baseball is all Brooks Calbert Robinson, Junior, ever wanted to do. Once, when he was a kid in junior high school, the students were asked to write a composition on what they wanted to be when they grew up. Brooks wrote that he wanted to be a major league baseball player. He got an A on the paper!

Born in Little Rock, Arkansas, on May 18, 1937, Brooks was still a toddler when his dad, Brooks senior, began teaching him to catch a rubber baseball. Mr. Robinson worked as a firefighter but he had also played a lot of semi-professional baseball and had been a star softball player. He passed his love of baseball on to Buddy, as Brooks was called by the family. Between shifts at the fire station, Mr. Robinson would play catch, throw batting practice, and hit grounders for Buddy to field for hours.

When his dad wasn't around, little Brooks played baseball with his friends. When his friends weren't around, he played by himself. He would play catch off the front stoop or hit

> **CAREER HIGHLIGHTS:** His .971 fielding average is the best ever for a third baseman; won 16 straight Gold Glove awards for fielding excellence; played in the All-Star Game for 18 straight years; voted American League Most Valuable Player in 1964; named MVP of World Series in 1970.

rocks into the meadow with broomstick bats. Softball was big in Little Rock when he was a kid, so Brooks's first experience with organized ball was on his elementary school's softball team. He played catcher and in the infield.

By the time he reached Little Rock Central High School, Brooks was an all-around athlete. He was named to the all-state basketball team and ran the 880-yard race in track. He might have been a football star, too, but he gave up the sport after he quarterbacked his ninth-grade team to a state championship. He wanted to be a baseball player, so he decided that he had better not risk hurting himself on the football field.

Little Rock Central High had no baseball team, so Brooks started playing American Legion ball when he was 14. Soon he had big-league scouts going out of their way to watch him play. His team won the Arkansas State Legion championship in 1953 and made it to the finals the next year.

Scouts were impressed with Brooks's fancy fielding at third base and while they liked his throwing arm, they didn't think much of his speed.

When they finally offered him a contract, it was for just $4,000 a year! The University of Arkansas, meanwhile, offered him a full scholarship to play baseball and basketball. Brooks had a tough decision to make: pro baseball or college.

LITTLE-KNOWN FACT:
Although he is one of the greatest defensive third basemen of all time, Brooks once made three errors in one inning. In a game against the Oakland Athletics in 1971, Brooks fielded a bunt and threw the ball wildly, then booted a grounder and threw *it* wildly.

Although his parents had hoped he would go to college, they didn't pressure Brooks. They pointed out that few boys get a chance at a four-year scholarship and how hard it would be to make it to the big leagues, but they let him make up his own mind.

Brooks stuck with his childhood dream of becoming a pro baseball player. In June, 1955, at age 18, he reported to the Orioles' minor league team in York, Pennsylvania. Brooks batted .331 and drove in 67 runs in 95 games at York. The Orioles were impressed and called him up to Baltimore in September. He had two hits in his first major league game and then went 0 for 18! He spent most of 1956 and part of 1957 back in the minors.

By 1958, Brooks had become the starting third baseman for the Baltimore Orioles. But he batted only .238 in 145 games and when the 1959 season started, he found himself back in the minors. He didn't stay long though! Sent to a Pacific Coast League team in Vancouver, British Columbia,

Canada, Brooks hit .331 in 42 games and was recalled to the Orioles. He batted a respectable .284 in 88 games that season. Finally, at 22, he had arrived as a major leaguer!

Brooks became one of the best players in the American League in 1960. He hit .294 with 14 home runs and 88 RBIs as the Orioles finished second. He also led the league's third basemen in put-outs, assists, and fielding percentage. In 1962, his numbers climbed to .303 with 23 homers and 86 RBIs.

In 1964, Brooks enjoyed the best season of his career. He batted .317, slammed 28 home runs, and drove in a league-leading 118 RBIs — all career highs. Even though the Orioles finished in third place, Brooks was named the American League's Most Valuable Player. Brooks appeared in the All-Star Game for the fifth year in a row and won his fifth Gold Glove, but something was missing. Brooks wanted the team to win.

After Frank Robinson, a hard-hitting outfielder (but no relation to Brooks), was acquired from the Cincinnati Reds before the 1966 season, winning came along, too. The Orioles played in — and won — their first World Series! Frank won the Triple Crown of batting (highest batting average, home run, and RBI totals) and was named the league's MVP. But Brooks had a great year, too. In addition to his stellar fielding, he had 23 homers and 100 RBIs during the regular season. He smashed a home run in the first inning of the first game of the World Series as the O's

> **WHEN** Cal Ripken Jr. was 10 years old in 1970, Brooks Robinson was 33 and one of baseball's biggest stars. He was named the Most Valuable Player in the World Series after leading the Baltimore Orioles to the championship.

swept the Los Angeles Dodgers in four games.

The "Frank and Brooks Show" led the Orioles to three straight American League pennants from 1969 to 1971. In 1969, Brooks hit only .234 but it seemed that every one of his hits knocked in an important run. He ended up with 23 homers and 84 RBIs. The Orioles beat the Minnesota Twins in the first American League Championship Series since 1897 and were heavy favorites to beat the upstart New York Mets in the World Series. Brooks batted .053 and the "Miracle Mets" stunned everyone by winning in five games.

BROOKS SAID: "Fifty years from now I'll just be three inches of type in a record book, but I hope I'll stand a lot taller than that to [my wife] Connie and my kids."

The Orioles were determined to win the next year, and no player was more determined than Brooks. With Brooks knocking in 94 runs, the Orioles won 108 games to win the A.L. Eastern Division by 15 games. They swept the Twins in the ALCS to advance to the World Series against the Cincinnati Reds. The Reds, who would go on to win two world championships, in 1975 and 1976, had standout players Pete Rose, Johnny Bench, and Tony Perez.

The Orioles had Brooks. At the plate, he went 9 for 21 (for a .429 average) with two homers, two doubles, and six RBIs. In the field, he went beyond his "vacuum cleaner" reputation, making acrobatic stops and turning "sure hits" into routine outs. The Orioles won in five games and Brooks was named the Series' Most Valuable Player. Film clips of his play in that Series are shown nearly every October when the World Series comes around because his performance still ranks as one of the greatest in the history of the game.

Baltimore won the pennant again in 1971. Brooks drove in 92 runs and hit 20 homers during the regular season, and hit .364 as the O's swept the Oakland A's in the playoffs. He hit .318 and led the team with five RBIs in the World Series, but the Pittsburgh Pirates won in seven games.

The 1971 World Series was Brooks's last. It was also the last year in which he hit double figures in home runs.

> **OTHERS SAID:** "He plays third base like he came down from another league." — *Ed Hurley, American League umpire.*

He played six more seasons and helped the Orioles to A.L. East titles in 1973 and 1974.

When Brooks retired during the 1977 season, he had hit 268 home runs and driven in 1,357 runs in 2,896 big-league games. No major league third baseman had ever played as many games, made as many put-outs (2,697), as many assists (6,205), or turned as many double plays (618). He had won 16 consecutive Gold Gloves for fielding. And he had batted .289 in All-Star Games and .303 in the playoffs and World Series. He was an easy selection to the Baseball Hall of Fame six years later.

Brooks continues to keep an apartment in the Baltimore area with his wife, Connie, and is now a color commentator for Orioles television broadcasts. When the All-Star Game was played in Baltimore in July 1993, the "Brooks and Frank Show" made a return appearance when the two men acted as honorary managers of the American League team. Brooks drew as big an ovation as anybody there — except, perhaps, Cal Ripken, Junior.

CHAPTER SIX

★ SHAQUILLE O'NEAL ★ AND HIS HERO: KAREEM ABDUL-JABBAR

Shaquille O'Neal, the 7' 1", 301-pound center for the Orlando Magic, is one of the biggest men in basketball. He is strong, quick, and jumps well. All these things make Shaquille [sha-KEEL] one of the most feared and respected players in the National Basketball Association (NBA).

At the same time, Shaquille has a sunny, fun-loving personality. He seems to enjoy himself wherever he is. And that makes him one of the players fans love most in the NBA.

When he was a kid, Shaq was ashamed of his size. He grew to 6' 8" in high school, and he wasn't well-coordinated. He used to slouch to try to make himself look smaller. "My parents told me to be proud," he recalls, "but I wasn't. I wanted to be normal."

Basketball fans everywhere are happy that Shaq wasn't "normal." Since getting serious about basketball, he has earned a scholarship to Louisiana State University, where he was named college player of the year, and become one of the dominant players in the NBA, easily winning Rookie of the Year honors for the 1992–93 season.

Shaquille was born on March 6, 1972 in Newark, New

As a kid, Shaq was ashamed of his size. As an adult, he's made good use of it in the NBA!

BARRY GOSSAGE

Jersey. His mother wanted to give her son a special name. She chose an Islamic name, Shaquille Rashaun, which means "little warrior" in Arabic. At birth, Shaquille was given his mother's last name because his parents were not yet married. His father, Philip Harrison, joined the Army and was sent overseas before he could marry his sweetheart, Lucille O'Neal. As soon as the Army allowed, Mr. Harrison returned and married Shaquille's mother. But he insisted that Shaquille keep his mother's last name because Mrs. Harrison had no brothers or nephews to carry on the O'Neal family name.

Shaquille got some of his talent from his 6' 5" father, who had played basketball in college. Mr. Harrison eventually became a staff sergeant in the Army and the family lived on a number of Army bases when Shaq was young. It was a mixed blessing. "The best part for me was just getting out of the city," Shaquille told *The New York Times* in 1992. "In the city I come from, there are a lot of temptations: drugs, gangs. . . . The worst part was, like traveling, you know? Meeting people, getting tight with them, and then having to leave."

While the family was living in Germany, Shaquille went to a basketball clinic on the base given by Dale Brown, the head coach at LSU. Coach Brown thought Shaq, who was already 6' 8" tall, was in the Army. When he found out that Shaq was only 13, he suggested that he might someday play for LSU.

But Shaq was having trouble making his school team! He was cut from his ninth-grade team because he wasn't athletic enough. "I couldn't jump over a pencil," he said. "I had to practice." He practiced a lot. He also did exercises to strengthen his knees, ankles, and thighs. His dad worked with him, teaching him some moves.

By the time he entered 10th grade, Shaq was good enough to make the school team. His favorite players were Kareem Abdul-Jabbar and Julius Erving, but his dad told him not to get carried away with hero-worship. He said Shaq should not try to be like any other player. Instead, he should develop his own style of play.

"That stuck with me," Shaq said. "I didn't want to try to be somebody else. I wanted my own identity. I wanted to be a complete player. An aggressive player. One who hustles all the time. One who is sportsmanlike. And, most of all, one who is a winner." Shaq still looked up to Kareem, and tried to learn from watching him, but he used those lessons in his own way.

In 1987, when Shaquille was 15, his father was transferred to San Antonio, Texas. Shaq attended Cole High School. During his two years at Cole, Shaq wore number 33 in honor of Kareem. His team went 68–1!

Shaquille then went to LSU to play for Coach Brown. He continued to wear Kareem's number and was delighted when Coach Brown invited Kareem to

SHAQ SAYS: "I know there are a lot of expectations. If I become a great center like Wilt Chamberlain or Bill Russell or Kareem Abdul-Jabbar or Bill Walton, that's good. If not, I'll live a happy life and keep a smile."

come to Louisiana to work with Shaquille. Kareem showed Shaq the basics of the "skyhook," a special hook shot for which Kareem was famous.

At LSU, Shaq became a national star, averaging 21.6 points and 13.5 rebounds per game over his college career. He earned All-America honors twice. But he was discouraged by the way less capable players on opposing teams ganged up on him, and disappointed by his team's lack of success. After three seasons, Shaquille quit college and joined the NBA. He promised his parents that he would someday get his college diploma. In the spring of 1992, Shaq became the Number 1 pick in the NBA Draft and signed a seven-year, $41 million contract with the Orlando Magic.

Today, with the retirement of Michael Jordan, Shaquille is a big man who has become one of the big names in the NBA.

★ KAREEM ABDUL-JABBAR ★

As a kid and in college, he was known as Lew Alcindor. Later, he was Kareem Abdul-Jabbar. By any name, this man was one of the most influential players in the history of basketball. He was a legend on the court for more than three decades. He was also a socially-conscious athlete, a man of intense pride who stood up for his beliefs, even though it angered millions of people.

Kareem also studied Arabic at Harvard University and collected Oriental rugs and jazz records. But it was being the dominant center in basketball for nearly 20 years that kept Kareem in the limelight.

In the history of pro basketball, three players have had the greatest impact on the center position: Bill Russell (1956–1969), Wilt Chamberlain (1959–1973), and Kareem. Kareem was a combination of both men. He had the grace, finesse, and defensive instincts of Bill and the intimidating height, scoring ability, and offensive explosiveness of Wilt. Kareem scored more points (38,387) than anyone in NBA history. He also was named the league's Most Valuable Player (MVP) six times. Some say he was the greatest player of all time, although it's hard to compare talent of different eras.

Kareem was the ultimate team player — and winner. In high school, at Power Memorial Academy in New York City, his team lost only one game from 1963 to 1965. In college at the University of California at Los Angeles (UCLA), he led the Bruins to three straight NCAA championships. His pro career was even more remarkable. He played on six NBA championship teams, and twice was named MVP of the NBA Finals.

Kareem was born Ferdinand Lewis Alcindor, Junior, on April 16, 1947, in New York City. He was big even at birth, weighing 12 pounds, 11 ounces and measuring 22½ inches. His father made his living as a bill collector and, later, as a sergeant with the Transit Authority's police department. But Mr. Alcindor was also an accomplished trombone player. Music was always being played in the Alcindor household. When Lewis was 5, his father graduated from the Juilliard

Kareem scored more points than anyone in NBA history.

School of Music, one of the best music schools in the country.

Lewis's mother also had a great interest in music, as well as in education. There were always lots of books around the Alcindor household. Lewis was 9 years old when he realized he was much better at something than most kids his age, and it wasn't basketball. It was reading! He was in the fourth grade at Holy Providence School, a Catholic boarding school in Cornwells Heights, Pennsylvania, that was filled mostly with poor, inner-city kids. Lewis went there for one year.

Lewis's reading ability created some problems for him because the other kids, who weren't fortunate enough to grow up in houses filled with books, resented it.

> **Name:** Kareem Abdul-Jabbar (born Ferdinand Lewis Alcindor, Junior)
> **Nickname:** "Cap"
> **Born:** April 16, 1947, New York City
> **Height:** 7' 2"   **Weight:** 267 lbs.
> **Cool fact:** Kareem was not just a good basketball player. He was also a powerful runner, swimmer, bicycle racer, and tennis player.

"These other black kids had come from families where reading was regarded as some kind of occult art," he told *Sports Illustrated* in 1969. "They were all too busy trying to keep from being hungry and miserable to spend any time on books, and this, too, is part of the black condition."

After the nuns had this fourth-grader read for the seventh-graders, Lewis found it hard to make friends. "They thought I was some kind of weird egghead, and I'm anything but an egghead," he said. "And they shunned me."

Once basketball season started, however, the students approached Lewis differently. "I was tall, about a head taller than the other guys in the fourth grade, and so the kids hustled me out to the playground to teach me the game from scratch — and claw, and elbow," Lewis told *Sports Illustrated*. "They played a tough fundamental game, sort of a blend of basketball, lacrosse, and prizefighting.

"From that point on — I was 9 years old and 5' 4" tall — the pattern of my life was set. I operated on a cycle, and the cycle was based on the basketball season. For me, that was the season and all life revolves around it, like a biological clock."

Back in New York, Lewis gradually learned how to play basketball well. He worked on his moves daily. By the time he was 14, he stood 6' 8" and many high schools were trying to recruit him. He chose to attend Power Memorial Academy. In his three years on the varsity, he scored 2,067 points and grabbed 2,002 rebounds. The team once won 71 straight games!

By his senior year in high school, Lewis had grown to be 7' 1" tall. Sixty colleges tried to recruit him, especially because he was a solid student as well as an exceptional basketball player. He chose UCLA. As far as basketball was concerned, it turned out to be a great decision. With the help of UCLA's legendary coach, John Wooden, and a fine group of teammates, Lewis became the dominant force in college basketball. He perfected a hook shot no one could stop (later dubbed a "skyhook" by an announc-

CAREER HIGHLIGHTS: Two-time college basketball Player of the Year at UCLA (1967, 1969); named Most Outstanding Player of NCAA Tournament three times (1967–69); named MVP six times during NBA career; named MVP of NBA Finals twice; all-time leading scorer in the NBA with 38,387 points.

er). During Lew's three years on the UCLA team (freshman weren't allowed to play varsity sports then), the Bruins lost only two games and won three straight NCAA championships. Each year he was named the Most Outstanding Player of the tournament.

But it was a turbulent time off the court for Lew. During his years at college (1966–69), the Black Power movement was at its peak in this country and a number of blacks were turning to the Islamic religion, which preaches acceptance of all people, for guidance. Lew, who was raised a Catholic, was intrigued.

WHEN Shaquille O'Neal was 10 years old in 1982, Kareem Abdul-Jabbar was 35 and helped lead the Los Angeles Lakers to the NBA title. During the regular season, Kareem was sixth in the league in scoring (23.9 points per game), third in blocked shots (2.72), and fourth in shooting percentage (.579).

In November of his junior year at UCLA, Lewis changed his life dramatically. He met with Harry Edwards, a black activist leader, to discuss asking all African-American athletes to boycott the 1968 Summer Olympics, which were to be held in Mexico City, Mexico. The boycott didn't happen, but Lew stayed away from the Games, anyway. He believed he could contribute more for the black youth of the country if he worked on the city playgrounds rather than go compete for a gold medal, which the United States was almost certain to win anyway. (It did.) He also didn't want to jeopardize his chances of graduating on time from UCLA because of all the travel and practice time.

Lew's decision angered many Americans, who felt he was a traitor for not playing for his country. Lew stood by his decision and returned to New York to work with youth on the playgrounds. Then something else happened.

A few years earlier, Lew had read a book about a black power leader named Malcolm X, who had changed his life for the better after joining the Islamic faith, becoming what is called a Black Muslim. Lew decided to investigate Islam himself. He studied it carefully and, late that summer, became a Sunnite Muslim. He was given a new name: Kareem Abdul-Jabbar. It is

> **KAREEM SAID:** "There's a certain 'otherness' about me. That makes it hard for me. I'm not a mainstream type of person. I'm an individual and that, I think, should be something in my favor because this is a nation of individuals. The American spirit is the spirit of the individual. We guarantee freedom, encourage freedom of expression and I've expressed myself. That's a positive thing."

an Arabic name which means "generous and powerful servant of Allah." (Allah is Arabic for God.) He returned to UCLA that fall a new person, although he did not make it public that he had a new name.

On the court, Lew/Kareem was still a force. He averaged 24 points and 14.7 rebounds as the Bruins won their third straight national college title.

Kareem joined the Milwaukee Bucks for the 1969–70 NBA season. He was an immediate force in the league and won Rookie of the Year honors, just as Shaquille would 23 years later.

In 1971, after acquiring the great guard Oscar Robertson to complement Kareem, the Bucks won the NBA championship and Kareem earned his first MVP award. In June 1971,

Kareem announced his conversion to Islam. "I never had any real trouble passing my change off on the public," Kareem said. "Because of my talent on the basketball court, people tended to avoid engaging me in any conflict if they could help it. The people in Milwaukee were good about it. They realized I wasn't some sort of idiot."

> **OTHERS SAID:** "You just have to say he's remarkable, a remarkable once-in-a-lifetime athlete, one of the most durable that's ever played — more durable than anybody psychologically, because that's what keeps guys going. He's a proud man." — *Pat Riley, former coach of the Lakers.*

The Bucks won at least 60 games in each of the next two seasons and made it to the Finals in 1974, before losing to the Boston Celtics.

When Kareem's contract expired in 1975, he tried to get back to the city he knew best. He wanted to play for the New York Knicks. But when a trade couldn't be worked out with New York, Kareem settled on Los Angeles, which traded two players and the draft rights to two others to the Bucks for him.

With Kareem, the Lakers thrived. Kareem earned five more NBA championship rings and three more league MVP awards. After Magic Johnson joined them in 1979, they became *the* powerhouse team of the 1980's and one of the most exciting pro basketball teams of all time.

When Kareem retired after the 1988–89 season, he was 42 years old. He holds many of the NBA's career records, including most points, most blocked shots, most field goals, most games, and most minutes. For all those basketball fans who saw this giant of a man play, they were minutes well-spent.

CHAPTER SEVEN

JOHN ELWAY AND HIS HERO: ★ ROGER STAUBACH ★

When it comes to late-game heroics and heart-stopping comebacks, John Elway of the Denver Broncos is the most exciting quarterback in the National Football League. A game is almost never over when John has the ball!

In his first 10 years with the Broncos, John helped his team come from behind to win 24 times in the fourth quarter. He has done it in playoff games and in American Football Conference Championship Games. In the process, he has led Denver to three Super Bowl appearances.

Part of John's success comes from his ability both to run with the ball and to pass it. He is the only quarterback in NFL history to pass for 3,000 or more yards and rush for at least 200 yards in seven straight seasons. His career 2,435 yards as of the end of the 1993 season put him in the top 10 on the all-time NFL quarterback rushing list. At the same time, he's famous for his long passes: He has completed more than 40 "bombs" of 50 or more yards!

John is big at 6' 3" and 215 pounds, yet he is quick on his feet. His arm is his trademark, however. Few quarterbacks throw the ball harder than John does. He throws the ball so

John was a running back in the fifth grade, but then his dad suggested he try playing quarterback.

hard that it can leave a mark on his receivers' chests.

John remembers having a strong arm even as a kid growing up in the state of Washington. "We used to have dirt-clod fights and snowball fights, and everybody wanted to be on my side because I threw the dirt clods and snowballs so hard," John told *Sports Illustrated For Kids* magazine.

John wasn't always a quarterback. As a fifth-grader, he was the star running back of his youth-league team. Then his family moved to another town and John couldn't play football again until high school. John's father, Jack, who was the offensive coordinator for Washington State University's football team, suggested that John switch to quarterback.

In 1976, the family moved to Northridge, California. John made the varsity as a sophomore at Granada Hills High School and was starting by mid-season.

By his senior year, he was the best high school quarterback in the nation. Dozens of colleges recruited him and he chose to go to Stanford University. In his four years there, John threw more passes (1,243) and completed more passes (774) than any college quarterback before him.

JOHN SAYS: "There isn't one moment about Roger's career that stands out for me. There is a whole highlight reel!"

John also excelled in baseball. After his sophomore year he was drafted by the New York Yankees. In the summer of 1982 he played for their minor league team in Oneonta, N.Y. He did very well, but he knew his future was in football.

John was selected as the first pick in the 1983 NFL draft by the Baltimore Colts (now the Indianapolis Colts) but was traded to the Broncos. He had a poor rookie season but has been one of the best in the NFL ever since.

John reminds some fans of his boyhood hero, Roger Staubach, the Hall of Fame quarterback who helped lead the Dallas Cowboys to five Super Bowls in the 1970's.

"He was my role model," said John. "He stood for everything that's important: He was smart and he had the skills, but he also played hard. And he never gave up."

John turned pro in 1983 and met Roger in 1985. "There wasn't much conversation," says John. "But there sure was a twinkle in my eye."

71

★ ROGER STAUBACH ★

Roger Staubach *[STAH-bock]* was like an old-time comic book hero: He had great physical abilities and a good head on his shoulders. He was clean-living and religious. And, of course, he could be counted on to save the day. He sounds too good to be true.

One of the greatest quarterbacks in football history, Roger was a gifted runner and a pinpoint passer. He won the 1963 Heisman Trophy as the best college player when he was a junior at the U.S. Naval Academy. Then, as a pro, he helped lead the Dallas Cowboys to five Super Bowl appearances and two victories in the 1970's. He retired in 1979 as the leading passer in NFL history. What really set Roger apart, though, was his unyielding competitive spirit. While some athletes don't do well under pressure, Roger proved over and over that he was at his very best when the game was on the line.

Born on February 5, 1942, Roger grew up in the Cincinnati, Ohio, suburb of Silverton. His father, Bob, was a shoe and leather salesman who worked hard but never made a lot of money. The Staubachs were devout Roman Catholics. Roger was an altar boy and attended a Catholic school.

Baseball and basketball were Roger's favorite sports as a kid. He began playing organized baseball at about age 7, and played football and basketball on Catholic Youth Organization teams beginning in the seventh grade. He soon realized that a kid could be something of a hero if he scored a touchdown, so Roger promptly became a hero by scoring 17 TDs as an eighth-grade running back!

By the time he reached Purcell High School, he was on the

varsity baseball and football teams, although he was more interested in football. He played end on the freshman football team and was later a defensive back for the varsity. When Roger became the starting quarterback his senior year, he would often run the ball, even if a pass play was called. That's when he first earned the nickname "Roger the Dodger."

A number of colleges wanted Roger to play for them. Rick Forzano, an assistant football coach at the U.S. Naval Academy, asked Roger to consider his school, and once Roger visited the Naval Academy in Annapolis, Maryland, he got

Roger became an NFL star despite not playing for four years in order to serve in the Navy.

WALTER IOSS / SPORTS ILLUSTRATED

interested. The Naval Academy is a special kind of college that trains students to become officers in the Navy and Marine Corps. It is tough academically and very strict. Although Roger was a good student, he had a hard time studying and he didn't score well enough on the verbal part of his college entrance exams to be admitted. He spent a year at the New Mexico Military Institute and then tried again. In the summer of 1961, Roger entered the Academy. He played football, baseball, and basketball there, becoming one of the best all-around athletes in the Academy's history. In three years, Roger earned seven varsity letters!

Name: Roger Thomas Staubach
Nickname: "Roger the Dodger"
Born: February 5, 1942, Silverton, Ohio
Height: 6' 3" **Weight:** 202 lbs.
Cool fact: In the 1961 Ohio High School All-Star game, Roger played mostly on defense and made close to a dozen tackles!

But it was Roger's performance on the football field that turned heads. At 6' 3" and 202 pounds, he was big and quick. Not only did he have a strong passing arm, but he was an excellent runner. He was especially good at escaping from would-be tacklers while trying to get off a pass.

In 1963, Roger won the Heisman Trophy and led Navy to a Number 2 national ranking. Navy lost to the University of Texas, 28–6, in the Cotton Bowl on New Year's Day, but Roger put on a display of his great talent as a quarterback.

During his three seasons at Navy, Roger collected a regular-season total of 4,253 yards passing and rushing. He set a school career record for quarterbacks by completing 63 percent of his passes. Despite these numbers, Roger couldn't join the pros right away because Academy students were required to spend four years in the Navy after they graduated.

No one had ever stopped playing competitive football for four years and returned to become a top-ranked pro quarterback. Most NFL teams didn't think that Roger could do it. But the Cowboys took a chance and drafted him anyway, in the 10th round.

Roger graduated from the Academy in 1965 and went on active duty in the Navy. He served one year in Vietnam during the Vietnam War. All the time he was in the Navy, Roger tried to keep himself in shape for football as best he could.

By July 1969, Roger had completed his Navy duty. He joined the Cowboys and spent two years learning the Cowboys' offensive system and improving his skills. In the middle of the 1971 season, at the ripe old age of

CAREER HIGHLIGHTS:
Heisman Trophy Winner, 1963; led NFL in passing in 1971, '73, '78, and '79; played in the Super Bowl four times, winning twice; led his team to comeback victories in the final two minutes or in overtime 14 times.

29, Roger finally got his chance to be a starting quarterback in the NFL—and he led the Cowboys all the way to the Super Bowl championship! That season, Roger led the NFC in passing. He also ran the ball 41 times and averaged 8.4 yards per carry. In the Super Bowl, the Cowboys beat the Miami Dolphins, 24–3, and Roger was named the Most Valuable Player. Roger had been well worth waiting for!

The next season, Roger suffered a shoulder separation in a preseason game and didn't start the rest of the season. But he came off the bench to rally Dallas to a 30–28 victory over the

San Francisco 49ers in the playoffs. His performance earned Roger the reputation of being a miracle worker.

In that game, the Cowboys were trailing, 28–16, with just under two minutes remaining in the fourth quarter. Roger had come in late in the third quarter to replace starting quarterback Craig Morton. Roger guided the Cowboys 55 yards down the field to a touchdown in just 32 seconds. Then the Cowboys recovered an onside kick at the 50-yard line and Roger went to work again. In three stunning plays—a 21-yard run and two sharp passes by Roger—the Cowboys found the end zone and scored the winning touchdown! Although the Cowboys lost to the Washington Redskins, 26–3, in the National Football Conference championship the next week, Roger had regained his position as the regular starter once and for all.

WHEN John Elway was 10 years old in 1970, Roger Staubach was 28 and in his second professional season with the Dallas Cowboys. He didn't get a chance to become the team's starting quarterback until the next year.

In 1973, Roger led the NFL in passing for the second time. And again the Cowboys were beaten in the NFC title game, losing to the Minnesota Vikings.

Despite ankle and rib injuries, Roger set a club record for completed passes in 1974, but the Cowboys missed the playoffs for the only time during his career.

Then came 1975, Roger's finest season and the year he earned his place as the greatest quarterback in Cowboys' history. Once again, it was a dramatic comeback that amazed Roger's teammates, opponents, and fans alike.

In the closing seconds of a playoff game against the

Vikings in December 1975, Dallas was trailing, 14–10. The Cowboys had the ball, but they had a fourth down with 16 yards to go on their 25-yard line. Roger passed 25 yards to receiver Drew Pearson for a first down. On the next play, he threw 50 yards to Drew, who caught the ball at the five-yard line. Drew then dashed into the end zone for the winning touchdown!

The Cowboys went on to the Super Bowl that season and lost, 21–17, to the Pittsburgh Steelers. Roger had rallied the team for a 23-yard drive in the last minute and a half, and almost threw a game-winning touchdown pass on the last play of the game. The pass, however, was intercepted in the end zone!

Roger's reputation as a great quarterback and an incredible comeback player continued to grow. Over the next four seasons, he led the Cowboys to two

ROGER SAID: "You know how you can go to a game and you can just kind of pick out the kids who are the competitive types? I feel fortunate that I was that way."

more NFC Championship Game appearances and two more Super Bowls. Dallas beat the Denver Broncos to win the Super Bowl after the 1977 season. The Cowboys then lost the big game to the Steelers the following year. Win or lose, Roger created excitement inall four of the Super Bowl games in which he started.

The 1979 season was Roger's last, and he left the fans with something to remember. Four times he rallied the Cowboys to victory in the final two minutes. In the last game of the regular season, he sparked two touchdown drives in the closing minutes to beat the Washington Redskins, 35–34, and clinch the division title. For the third time in his career, he led the NFL in passing rating.

The Cowboys' season ended abruptly with a loss in a divisional playoff game the next week. Roger's career ended three months later when he decided to retire for medical reasons. Roger had suffered five concussions (head injuries) during the 1979 season, and a doctor told him that it was too dangerous to continue playing. Roger was 38 years old.

> **OTHERS SAID:** "Roger Staubach just isn't a guy you tell he can't do something. There's no such word as 'can't' to him. You tell him that and he'll go right out and prove you're wrong." — *Mike Ditka, Hall of Fame player and former NFL coach.*

In his 11 NFL seasons, he completed 1,685 passes for 22,700 yards. He also rushed for a career total of 2,264 yards, an average of 5.5 yards per carry. In his last seven seasons as the regular starting quarterback, the Cowboys won 74 games and lost only 28 in the regular season. They were never shut out.

Roger stayed in Dallas and formed his own real estate company. In 1985, the first year he was eligible, he was inducted into the Pro Football Hall of Fame. There are a lot of great quarterbacks in the Hall. But at least one expert, a Hall of Famer himself, wouldn't trade Roger Staubach for any of them.

"I don't know of any quarterback I've played against or watched that I would rather have than Roger," said Tom Landry, who coached the Cowboys from 1960 to 1988.

For all the people who played or worked with Roger at Navy and Dallas, he really was too good to be true.

CHAPTER EIGHT

★ PATRICK EWING ★ AND HIS HERO: PELÉ

As a boy, Patrick Ewing never dreamed that he would someday become one of the best centers in the National Basketball Association. Growing up in Jamaica, an island in the Caribbean, he didn't even know how to play basketball! Soccer was his sport and his hero was soccer star Pelé of Brazil.

Patrick, who played goalie as a kid in Jamaica, never got to see Pelé play in person, but after he grew up and became a famous athlete himself, he did meet his hero in a restaurant in New York City in the mid-1980's.

By that time, playing soccer was a thing of the past for Patrick. His life had changed direction when his parents decided they wanted a better life for their seven children than they could get in Jamaica. So, in 1971, Patrick's mother traveled to the United States and got a job in the cafeteria at Massachusetts General Hospital in Cambridge. Two years later, she had enough money so that her husband could come. The kids, including 12-year-old Patrick, came shortly afterward. Patrick's dad got a job in a factory making rubber hoses.

Basketball was the favorite sport in Patrick's new neighborhood. One day, while he was watching a game on the play-

MANNY MILLAN / SPORTS ILLUSTRATED

Patrick didn't handle a basketball until he was 12, and now he's an expert!

ground, a group of kids asked him if he wanted to play. Because he was so tall, the kids figured Patrick must be naturally good. Having never handled a basketball before, he was awkward and clumsy, and the kids teased him.

But Patrick wanted to be good at the game, so he worked night and day at it. He also grew. By the time he was in 11th grade, Patrick was 6' 11" tall. By his senior year, he was 7 feet tall! The kids had stopped teasing him and Patrick became a dominant player at Cambridge's Rindge & Latin High School. During his four years on the varsity, Rindge & Latin won 94 of 99 games and three Massachusetts state championships!

After becoming a U.S. citizen in 1980, Patrick became the first high school student ever invited to try out for the U.S. Olympic basketball team. He didn't make the 1980 team, but four years later, he proudly helped the States win the gold medal at the 1984 Olympics in Los Angeles. He also was on the "Dream Team" that won the gold at the 1992 Games in Barcelona, Spain.

Back in high school, though, life wasn't easy for Patrick. Because of his Jamaican accent, he sometimes had a hard time being understood. But he worked hard and, by graduation, he had earned a reputation for both his basketball *and* his classroom abilities. "He was a great student because he would ask questions. And if he didn't understand the answer, he would ask again," said Patrick's high school coach, Michael Jarvis.

PATRICK SAYS: "Pelé was a great soccer player. And I wanted to be a soccer player just like him."

Patrick's talent earned him a basketball scholarship to Georgetown University in Washington, D.C.There, he continued to work hard in class and on the court, and it showed. He led the Georgetown Hoyas to the National Collegiate Athletic Association Division I championship three times in four years. In 1984, Patrick's junior year, the Hoyas won 34 of 37 games and won the NCAA title. Patrick earned a degree in Fine Arts in 1985.

The New York Knicks made Patrick the first pick in the 1985 NBA Draft. He has been one of the best centers in the NBA ever since, averaging more than 23 points per game. He has made the All-Star team seven times.

Still, as good as Patrick is, he hopes to be a better player. "I want to improve my passing and my rebounding," he says. "I want to be a better all-around player."

Like his boyhood idol Pelé, Patrick knows that nothing leads to success faster than hard work.

★ PELÉ ★

We've all heard rags-to-riches stories. You know, poor boy makes good, gets rich, earns fame. That sounds like the story of Pelé's life. In fact, the man who is known as the greatest soccer player in history first played using a bundle of rags for a ball.

But Pelé was more than one of the greatest, richest, and most successful athletes of all time. He became a legend among legends. He was the King of Soccer, or simply the King, as he was often called. He was so admired and beloved that Brazil declared him a national treasure. Hotels around the world put up plaques in rooms he had stayed in that said, "Pelé slept here." And once, in 1969, a war between the African nations of Nigeria and Biafra was stopped for two days so that both sides could watch a soccer match in which Pelé was playing!

"He has done more goodwill than all the ambassadors of the world put together," a Brazilian ambassador to the United States once said. And he was probably right.

Pelé earned his reputation with his skill on the soccer field. Only Pelé has played on three World Cup championship teams. Only Pelé and two others have scored more than 1,000 goals as pro players. In addition to being able to score goals, he had unique skills as a passer and playmaker and an ability to motivate his teammates. Most of all, though, he brought excitement to the game. There are many who believe no athlete has been more entertaining or showed more joy in playing.

Pelé's real name is Edson Arantes do Nascimento and he was born on October 23, 1940, in the city of Três Corações, in the state of Minas Gerais in Brazil. His mother called him

"Dico," but around the time he was 8, he started to be called "Pelé" by the neighborhood children. It is a nickname he didn't like much and still doesn't understand.

"It really has no meaning as far as I can determine," Pelé once said. "I tried to find out over the years what it meant, but I never did. The kids started calling me that when I was little and I would fight them every time I heard it."

After he became famous as Pelé, he started to sign his autographs: "Edson = Pelé." And he fully expected to be known as

Pelé was called a "boy wonder" in soccer at age 15, and never lost his magic touch.

Edson once his playing career was over. No chance. Pelé has become one of the most recognizable names in the world.

Pelé was practically raised on soccer. When he was barely old enough to walk, he started kicking around a bundle of rags, which served as his first soccer ball. His father, Dondinho, was a professional soccer player, and a good one. He still holds the Brazilian record for most goals scored by headers (balls hit off the head) in one game, with five. But pro soccer players did not make very much money at that time. Although he was one of his team's best players, Dondinho earned just $4.50 a game!

When Pelé was 6 years old, his family moved to Baurú in the state of São Paulo. Dondinho played as a center-forward for the Baurú Athletic Club. Life was hard and the family was very poor, but it didn't bother little Edson. "We played from dawn to dusk," he recalled, "and the game we played was soccer."

Pelé's mother wasn't pleased with this schedule. "My mother was very disappointed in me as a young boy," Pelé said. "I was always cutting school and my mother wanted me to get an education. To make her happy, I

Name: Edson Arantes do Nascimento
Nicknames: Pelé, The Black Pearl, The King
Born: October 23, 1940, Três Corações, Minas Gerais, Brazil
Height: 5' 9"   **Weight:** 165 lbs.
Cool fact: In 1966, a Brazilian university doctor examined Pelé's body. For three weeks, his head, arms, and legs were repeatedly wired so the doctors could take precise readings with an electrical meter. When they were done, the doctors declared their findings: "Whatever field of endeavor this man entered, be it physical or mental, he would be a genius."

studied to be a cobbler's apprentice but it was a waste of time. Soccer was all I cared for."

Pelé played for a local team called Sete de Setembro (Seventh of September) and at the age of 11, he caught the attention of a retired soccer player named Waldemar de Brito. Mister de Brito had been a member of Brazil's World Cup team in 1934 and he was impressed by Pelé's ability to dominate older, more experienced players. Mister de Brito decided to become Pelé's coach and formed a junior team called Baquinho. That was the first time that Pelé ever played on a team that wore uniforms.

Baquinho won the city junior championship for three straight years and Pelé was beginning to be talked about as a "boy wonder." When Pelé was just 15, Mister de Brito convinced his parents to let him join Santos F.C., a professional club. Pelé would be paid $5 a month!

Pelé arrived in Santos on June 8, 1956, for the start of what was to become the most brilliant professional soccer career ever. But his first league championship game was hardly special. Playing for the Juvenile (rookie) team, he missed a penalty kick that cost his team the title!

CAREER HIGHLIGHTS: One of only three players in history to score 1,000 goals, finishing his career with 1,282; holds record for most goals scored in a season (126); only person to play on three World Cup championship teams.

Two months later, on September 7, Pelé played his first game for the top Santos team. He entered the game as a substitute in the second half of an exhibition game against a São Paulo team and he scored a goal—the first of 1,282 he would score as a professional. In 1957, his first full year with Santos, Pelé scored a league-high 17 goals and the following year he was selected to the Brazilian team that would play in the 1958 World Cup in Sweden.

That's when Pelé became an international star. He was only 17 years old and an injury prevented him from playing until the quarterfinal round. Then he took over. In the quarterfinal against Wales, he scored the game's only goal. In the semifinal against France, he scored three times. In the final, against Sweden, he scored two more goals, leading Brazil to a 5–2 win and its first World Cup championship. It marked the beginning of Brazilian dominance of World Cup soccer—and Pelé's dominance of soccer. Period.

> **WHEN** Patrick Ewing was 10 years old in 1972, Pelé was 32 and scored 50 goals in a season for the 14th time in his career. Two years earlier, he had led Brazil to an unprecedented third World Cup title.

What was it that made him so great? He was only 5' 9" and kind of stocky. But he had lightning-fast speed, incredible reflexes, and a great sense of what to do with the ball and when to do it. He was also a fierce competitor who made himself and his teammates better players when the pressure was on. Even though he was often guarded by two or even three opponents, Pelé was able to score. In 1959, Pelé scored 126 goals in one season and became the most sought-after player in the world. Brazil was so concerned that he might leave to play for another country that in 1960 it officially named him a national treasure that could not be bought or sold.

Pelé stayed with Santos and prospered. He became one of

the richest athletes in the world and helped Brazil win World Cups again in 1962 and again in 1970. In 1962, he actually missed most of the games with a muscle pull but in 1970, he dominated. He scored six times in six games in the qualifying round and added four more goals in the tournament. His brilliant head goal in the final against Italy put Brazil ahead to stay.

> **PELÉ SAID:** "I don't believe there is such a thing as a born soccer player. Perhaps you are born with certain skills and talents but success is no accident. It is hard work, perseverance, learning, studying, sacrifice and, most of all, love of what you are doing that make you great."

But that was Pelé's last goal in World Cup competition. He retired from soccer in 1974 and refused to return to play for Brazil in the 1974 World Cup. That angered many Brazilians, but they eventually forgave him.

Pelé's retirement did not last very long. A businessman named Clive Toye convinced him to come to the United States and play for the New York Cosmos of the North American Soccer League (NASL). The league had started in 1968 but it wasn't getting very many spectators to its games because soccer was not very popular in the States. The NASL needed a big-name player to draw people. Mr. Toye convinced Pelé that he could make soccer popular in America.

Some of his friends thought he was making a mistake, but Pelé accepted the challenge and signed a three-year, $4.75 million contract with the Cosmos. Even though he was 34 years old, Pelé dominated the league. He led the Cosmos to the 1977 NASL title and earned Most Valuable Player honors.

As Mr. Toye predicted, Pelé had a huge impact on soccer

in the United States. Because he was willing to come to the States, other top players agreed to come, too. Large crowds gathered to see these stars from all over the world. When Pelé entered the league, attendance was only 7,930 per game. In his final season with the Cosmos, attendance was 14,640 per game. For the first time, Americans really did pay attention to soccer.

OTHERS SAID: When he met Pope Paul VI, Pelé was a little nervous about meeting the honored head of the Roman Catholic church. But the Pope said to him, "I am more nervous than you because I have been wanting to meet Pelé personally for a long time."

"I came here with a mission because I believed in soccer," Pelé said. "I believed that if I can show the game to the American people, they will love it, too. It is a game people play all over the world, and it is a game that pays no attention to race or religion or country. Because of this, it is a special game."

Pelé played his last game on October 1, 1977, before 75,646 fans at Giants Stadium in New Jersey. He played the first half for the Cosmos and the second half for Santos. Professional soccer in the States has struggled ever since that time. That doesn't make Pelé or other soccer fans happy, but it seems to show what a force Pelé was on the U.S. soccer scene.

Since retiring from soccer, Pelé has contributed much to the game. He ran soccer camps and clinics throughout the world until 1984, and has written a number of books. Five movies have been made about him, and six others have featured him.

But it is on the soccer field that Pelé was truly a star, and will remain so in the eyes of soccer fans everywhere.

CHAPTER NINE

JENNIFER CAPRIATI AND HER HERO: ★ CHRIS EVERT ★

Legend has it that Jimmy Evert called his daughter, Chris, one night in the early 1980's. Chris was then the Number 1-ranked tennis player in the world.

"Chrissie, I think I've finally found someone as talented as you," said Mr. Evert. He was referring to a girl he was coaching named Jennifer Capriati, who was 4 years old!

Mr. Evert was considered one of the best tennis instructors in the world for kids. He had started his daughter, Chris, on the road to success. He had one rule, though: He would not teach anyone younger than 5 years old.

Jennifer Capriati made him break that rule.

Jennifer was what is called a child prodigy in tennis. When she was 3 years old, she started picking up her mother's tennis racket. At age 4, she was playing against the ball machine and could handle long rallies on the tennis court.

At the time, Jennifer and her family were living in Spain, where her father had grown up. She had been born in the United States on March 29, 1976, but she and her parents moved back to Spain shortly after she was born. They then returned to the United States in 1980 in order to get a good education for Jennifer and her brother, Steven, and because Jennifer had shown such good potential in tennis. They settled in Lauderhill, Florida, where Jennifer could play tennis year-round. Her father, Stefano, also knew he would have to find a special coach to help Jennifer develop her talent. That's when he approached Jimmy Evert.

"I wanted her to start off with a wise man, a guy who has already been through all of this and knows the psychology it takes to work with a little girl," Mr. Capriati recalled.

Jennifer was the youngest American ever to turn pro, which she did at 13 years, 11 months.

DAVID WALBERG/SPORTS ILLUSTRATED

At first Jimmy Evert said "No," but after watching Jennifer perform, he changed his mind. He taught Jennifer exactly what he had taught his daughter Chris years earlier: Be patient and play a steady baseline game.

Jennifer competed in her first amateur tournament when she was 6 years old. Four years later, she won her first tournament, the U.S. indoor championship for girls 12 and under. She also won the girls' title at a junior tournament in Jacksonville, Florida, in the 14-and-under age group. She was only 10 years old!

As Jennifer developed, Jennifer's dad decided she

JENNIFER SAYS: "The first time I practiced with Chris, I was so nervous I couldn't keep the ball in the court. She must have thought I was soooo bad."

needed a new coach who could help her mental approach to the game. He selected Rick Macci [MAY-cee].

"The first time I saw her play, I thought she was the most talented young player that I'd ever seen in junior tennis," Coach Macci said. "The inner qualities of being a champion were already there. Her balance, her movement on the court, the way she prepared to hit the ball."

Most weekends Jennifer's father would drive her to Coach Macci's tennis academy in Haines, Florida. The trip took three and a half hours each way! At the academy, Jennifer practiced against top junior-level boys. Most of the boys were better players than Jennifer was, but she gradually caught up.

In March of 1988, at age 12, Jennifer became the youngest girl ever to win the United States Tennis Association (USTA) Girls 18 Hard Court Championship. Four months later, she won the USTA Girls 18 Clay Court title!

At age 13, Jennifer became the youngest player ever in the Wightman Cup, an annual team competition between the United States and Great Britain. She stunned the tennis world by beating 21-year-old Clare Wood, a member of Britain's 1988 Olympic team. Jennifer won the match in only 42 minutes, 6–0, 6–0! She also won the singles title at the U.S. Open junior division and the junior singles titles at the French and Italian Opens. Her family then moved to Wesley Chapel, Florida, so Jennifer could train at the Harry Hopman International Tennis Academy, a training facility for kids and adults where many pros have trained.

Jennifer turned pro at the age of 13 years, 11 months. Her first tournament was the Virginia Slims of Florida in the town of Boca Raton. That's the same town where Chris Evert lived. Chris had been one of Jennifer's supporters early on, and was one of the people who helped Jennifer adjust to the pressures of pro tennis. She told Jennifer to have fun and ignore the pressure. Chris could not attend Jennifer's first match as a pro, but she sent a telegram of encouragement.

Jennifer won her first pro match, beating a 28-year-old! She reached the finals of the tournament before losing to 19-year-old Gabriela Sabatini. Each day of the tournament, Chris called Jennifer from Colorado.

Jennifer has ranked among the top 10 players in the world since she turned pro. She has been compared to Chris Evert often by sports journalists but, as much as she likes and admires Chris, she wants to be known as her own person.

"I love Chris, she's my friend," said Jennifer. "But I want to be known as me."

That's an attitude Jennifer's hero can well understand!

★ CHRIS EVERT ★

She was called the "Ice Maiden" because of what appeared to be her cold, mechanical approach to tennis. Her concentration was fierce and she almost never smiled. She ignored the crowd. She hardly ever rushed the net. She simply moved along the baseline and used a two-fisted backhand and her incredible determination to beat opponent after opponent.

You can't argue with the results: The one thing Chris Evert did more than any other player of her era was *win*. In fact, few athletes have ever dominated a sport the way Chris dominated

---

By the time she retired in 1989, Chris had won 157 singles titles, including this one at Wimbledon.

HEINZ KLUETMEIER / SPORTS ILLUSTRATED

tennis during the 1970's and early 1980's. Chris started out in tennis at the age of 6. By the time Chris was 16, she was a tennis powerhouse. By the time she retired in 1989, she had won six U.S. Open singles championships, seven French Opens, three Wimbledons, and two Australian Opens, plus 139 other singles titles on the women's professional circuit.

Chris was the first female tennis player to win $1 million dollars in prize money. She won a total of just under $9 million by the time she retired. Because Chris was so popular with fans, she also earned a lot of money endorsing products like Converse sneakers and Wilson tennis rackets. All told, her income from endorsements is estimated to be nearly $30 million!

Despite her many victories and great wealth, Chris wasn't entirely happy during much of her professional career. She didn't like some of the things people wrote and said about her.

Name: Christine Marie Evert
Nicknames: "Chrissie," "Ice Maiden"
Born: December 21, 1954, Fort Lauderdale, Florida
Height: 5' 6" **Weight:** 125 lbs.
Cool fact: When Chris was in grade school, she wrote that she wanted to be a missionary, teacher, or social worker when she grew up. "I always wanted to help people," she said.

"It always bothered me [when they referred to me as cold and mechanical]," Chris told a reporter several years ago. "Because I'm cool on the court and unemotional on the surface, they think that carries over to my private life. But I'm very emotional, and I'm very outgoing to my friends."

Even Chris admitted that on the court, her behavior was another matter. "When I get out on the tennis court, I'm there for a job," she said. "That's my career. I'm a perfectionist. Whatever I do, I don't want to be mediocre in it. "

Christine Marie Evert was born in Fort Lauderdale, Florida, on December 21, 1954. She was the second of five children in a family whose main love was the game of tennis. Her father, Jimmy, managed and taught tennis at Fort Lauderdale's Holiday Park Tennis Center, one of Florida's largest tennis complexes. He had been a fairly good tennis player himself, winning the National Indoor Junior Championship in 1940. His wife, Colette, enjoyed the game. Chris has an older brother, Drew, a younger brother, John, and two younger sisters, Jeanne and Clare. The two boys both earned state rankings as tennis players. In 1973, Jeanne was the runner-up in the 16-and-under girls' national championship.

> **CAREER HIGHLIGHTS:**
> Winner of six U.S. Opens, seven French Opens, three Wimbledons, and two Australian Opens; ranked No. 1 in the world six years; won nearly $9 million on women's pro tour.

Chris was only 6 when her father noticed her hitting balls against a wall at the courts. He decided to give her lessons. She liked the game immediately and would often spend two and a half hours after school and eight hours on weekends on the courts! Her parents encouraged Chris's tennis development, but did not push her into the game.

"The idea of producing tennis champions was the furthest thing from our mind," said Mrs. Evert in 1972.

But tennis became an important part of Chris's life. "I was very insecure when I was young," she once said. "I was shy and introverted. When I went out on the tennis court, I could express myself. It was a way of getting reactions from people, like my father. I really admired my dad and put him on a pedestal, and I wanted his attention. Whether it's ego or insecurity or whatever, when you start winning and getting attention, you like it and that feeling snowballs. You start to feel good about yourself. You feel complete and proud of yourself."

When she was 15 years old and still an amateur, Chris began to make a name for herself by beating Margaret Smith Court in a tournament in Charlotte, North Carolina. Mrs. Court had just become the second woman in history to complete the Grand Slam of tennis by winning the U.S., British, French, and Australian titles all in one year.

WHEN Jennifer Capriati was 10 years old in 1986, Chris Evert was 32 and still one of the top players on the women's professional tennis circuit. Chris won the French Open for the seventh time that year.

In the winter of 1971, Chris won the Virginia Slims Masters tournament in St. Petersburg, Florida. In August, she was chosen to compete against Great Britain for the Wightman Cup in Cleveland, Ohio. She was the youngest player ever to compete on the team (up to that point). Chris beat Great Britain's best player, Virginia Wade, 6–1, 6–1, to give the United States the Cup!

Chris's popularity really soared that September when she played in the U.S. Open at Forest Hills, New York. She advanced all the way to the semifinals before losing to Billie Jean King. The defeat ended a string of 46 consecutive victories against some of the best players in the world but tennis fans were delighted by this talented 16-year-old.

Not everything was rosy, though. Like most adolescents, Chris had her problems. Once she joined the professional tour, she began having trouble balancing the highs and lows of her tennis life with everyday relationships. Although the fans loved Chris, many of the women on the circuit resented her. Her concentration was her most effective weapon on the court, but it made her seem unfriendly and aloof to the older players on the tour. She was often lonely. She traveled with her mother and spent most of her days in hotel rooms.

None of that affected Chris's tennis much, though. On her 18th birthday in December 1972, Chris turned professional. She became eligible to compete for prize money. In her first tournament as a pro, in Fort Lauderdale in March 1973, she won the first prize of $10,000! In 1974, she won her first major titles, the women's singles championship at the French Open and at Wimbledon, England's prestigious tournament. Over the course of her career, Chris would win 157 singles titles in total and be ranked Number 1 in the world for six years. In one period, from August 1973 to May 1979, she won 125 consecutive matches played on clay courts!

CHRIS SAID: "You hate to lose more than you love to win. I hated it [losing]. I think you have to have that. And you have to have an arrogance to maintain a high level of confidence. You know you're better than the other players because there are so many times when you're down, 5–3, in the third set and you don't get worried. You still know you're going to win. That's true arrogance."

During that time, Chris also started making headlines in some newspapers for her social life. When she became engaged to tennis star Jimmy Connors, who also won at Wimbledon in 1974, everyone wanted to know what sweet, well-behaved Chris Evert saw in that wild Jimmy Connors. Soon Jimmy and Chris both decided marriage was no good for either of their careers and they split up. They remain good friends to this day.

In 1979, Chris married John Lloyd, a British tennis player. They were divorced eight years later. In 1988, Chris married former U.S. Olympic team skier Andy Mill. A year later, she retired from competitive tennis and, in 1991, she gave birth to a son, Alexander James. Chris and her family live in Aspen, Colorado, and Boca Raton, Florida. Chris devotes a lot of her time to her family. She still does endorsements but is more involved in her new career as a tennis commentator on television. And she is aware of the influence she has had on many of the women she now watches on the women's pro tennis tour.

OTHERS SAID: "She concentrates to the last point. It makes her a champion. Even when she is losing she concentrates and doesn't give up." — *former tennis champion Margaret Smith Court.*

"I never sought to be a role model," Chris told *Sports Illustrated*, "but I was placed in the position. So you do the best you can with it. It's how you perform on the court and conduct yourself, and how you deal with defeat. Those are the qualities people should look at, not whether you're gay or how many guys you've dated. Certain things are just not important; they don't have to do with your character. Your character is revealed in how you handle stressful situations."

As Jennifer Capriati knows, no player was ever cooler on the court than Christine Marie Evert.

CHAPTER TEN

KIRBY PUCKETT AND HIS HERO: ★ ERNIE BANKS ★

K irby Puckett doesn't really look like a baseball player. His short, stocky build seems more suited to football.

But Kirby is a great example of the old saying, "You can't judge a book by its cover," for he is one of the most exciting players in the major leagues. Kirby has been the Minnesota Twins' star centerfielder since 1984. Although only 5' 9", he packs 220 pounds on his frame and is very strong. He has a wide neck, big shoulders, and thick thighs, which he built from years of weightlifting.

Through the 1993 season, Kirby had a lifetime batting average of .318. He won the 1989 American League batting title with a .339 average and has had a total of six .300-plus seasons. Kirby has also played in eight All-Star Games and was named Most Valuable Player of the 1993 game.

Kirby contributes wherever he is. In his first nine years in Minnesota, the team has twice won the World Series: In 1987, the Twins beat the St. Louis Cardinals in seven games and in 1991, they beat the Atlanta Braves in seven games.

In 1991, Kirby was the Most Valuable Player of the American League Championship Series (ALCS) after the

Kirby is a leader with his bat, his glove, his words, and his positive attitude.

Twins beat the Toronto Blue Jays in five games. In that series, he hit .429 with two home runs and six RBIs.

Kirby's most memorable moment came in the 1991 World Series. The Braves were leading the Series, three games to two, and Game 6 was tied 3–3 in the 11th inning. Kirby hit a pitch over the fence for the game-winning homer. The Twins went on to win the next game, too, capturing the Series.

Not only does Kirby lead with his bat and his glove (he has won six Gold Glove awards for fielding excellence), but he is a leader with his words and positive attitude, too. He has a warm smile and is always giving his teammates sound advice.

For as long as he can remember, Kirby has loved baseball. He grew up in Chicago, Illinois, the youngest of nine children born to William and Catherine Puckett. The family lived in a three-room apartment on Chicago's South Side.

"It was a bad neighborhood," says Kirby. "A lot of guys I grew up with are dead or in jail." Kirby was able to avoid getting mixed up with the wrong crowd because of his mother's watchful eye.

Kirby began lifting weights when he was 17, and it helped him develop into an outstanding athlete. He was an All-America third baseman as a senior in high school and earned a scholarship to Bradley University in 1980. However, his father died in the fall of Kirby's freshman year and, in order to be closer to home, Kirby transferred to Triton Junior College, near Chicago, the next year. In 1982, he batted .472 and led Triton to the Junior College World Series.

KIRBY SAYS: "I admired [Ernie Banks], I always wanted to be like him. The reason I liked him so much is that he was a great player who was ready every single day. That is what made him different."

Growing up in Chicago, Kirby idolized Ernie Banks, who played shortstop and first base for the Cubs from 1953 to 1971. Kirby remembers getting to meet his hero after he himself had become a star. They met in 1986, when Kirby was chosen to play in his first All-Star Game and Ernie was there.

"I just told him how much I respected him," Kirby said. "No matter how good I am, there's no way I'll ever be the kind of player he was. No way. It'll never happen."

There are a few fans in Minnesota who would disagree!

★ ERNIE BANKS ★

When he was a kid growing up in Dallas, Texas, Ernie Banks did not care much for baseball. In fact, his father had to bribe him with nickels and dimes to get Ernie to play catch with him in the backyard! It was a good investment by Mr. Banks: Ernie went on to become one of the greatest players in baseball history.

Ernie is one of only 14 players in the history of Major League Baseball to hit 500 or more home runs. During his 19-year major league career — all of it spent with the Chicago Cubs — he hit 512 home runs. Before he retired in 1971, he had slammed 40 or more homers in a season five times and hit three in a game on four occasions!

What makes Ernie even more special is the fact that he played shortstop for the first 8½ years of his career. Shortstops don't usually hit home runs. In fact, before Ernie came along, the most home runs ever hit by a big league shortstop in one season was 39! He hit 293 homers in those 8½ seasons as a shortstop before he switched over to first base for the rest of his career.

Ernie wasn't just a power-hitting shortstop, he was a good fielder as well. In 1958 and 1959, as a shortstop, he was named the Most Valuable Player in the National League (N.L.).

That's not bad, especially when you consider that he was 17 years old before he ever played a baseball game! When Ernie was 10 years old, his father, Eddie, tried to get him interested in baseball by buying him a couple of baseballs, and a glove for $2.98, which is what a decent glove cost in 1941. Mr.

Ernie started out as a kid who didn't like baseball, and ended up in the Hall of Fame!

NATIONAL BASEBALL LIBRARY AND ARCHIVE, COOPERSTOWN, N.Y.

Banks wanted to get his son interested in the game because he had played baseball with the Dallas Green Monarchs, a semi-professional team, for eight years in the 1920's.

Ernie, who was one of 12 children, was a good athlete, but he just wasn't interested in baseball.

"I was more interested in softball, football, track, swimming, and basketball," Ernie recalled. "But my father would bribe me to catch with him by giving me a nickel or sometimes a dime."

When Mr. Banks did get a bat into Ernie's hands, it was a sight to behold. Ernie simply smashed the ball — and a few other things.

"Drives off Ernie's bat broke so many windows in the neighborhood that we were always in trouble," his dad told *The Sporting News.* "He smashed so many windows that I was almost broke trying to pay for them. That is when I learned something new. I'd roll out tin cans, cut them to the size of the window and use them as replacements for the broken glass. Everything went just fine until the folks on the inside tried to look out the window, and then our little gag was ruined. You'll never know the number of tin windows we had in our home!"

Name: Ernest Banks
Nicknames: Ernie, "The Sunshine Kid," "Mr. Cub"
Born: January 31, 1931, Dallas, Texas
Height: 6' 1" **Weight:** 180 lbs.
Batted and Threw: right-handed
Cool fact: Ernie learned his U.S. geography from the long bus trips he took with the Colts semi-pro baseball team.

Ernie's first exposure to professional baseball came as a batboy for his dad's old team when Ernie was about 8 years old.

"He was so small his mother had to cut the store uniform they bought for him to about half its original size," said Mr. Banks. "He was the most batless batboy you ever saw. For he'd be playing catch with some of the players when he should have been doing his regular chores.

"But Ernie was such a happy-go-lucky kid nobody minded too much that he was spending more time playing than working," added Mr. Banks.

Still, softball — not baseball — was the game in which Ernie excelled as a youth. He attended Booker T. Washington High School in Dallas and was a standout athlete in every sport he played. In the fall, he played end and was captain of the football team. In the winter, he was captain and forward on the basketball team. And he ran the quarter-mile and high-jumped for the track team in the spring. Washington High didn't even have a baseball team.

In the summer of 1948, Ernie was playing softball one day on the high school field. A scout for the Colts, a semi-pro Negro league team based in Amarillo, Texas, came by and asked Ernie to join his team. (Until Jackie Robinson joined the Brooklyn Dodgers in 1947, major league teams did not hire black players. Instead, many black players joined Negro leagues.) Ernie was 17 years old and had never played a game of baseball in his life, but it didn't seem to matter. The scout figured that the skills Ernie had acquired playing softball were good enough. After getting his mother's permission, Ernie joined the team and spent the rest of the summer playing for the Colts. He was paid about $5 per game. And the scout was right: Ernie played well.

> **CAREER HIGHLIGHTS:** Hit 512 home runs, tied for 12th on the all-time list; named National League Most Valuable Player in 1958 and 1959, the first N.L. player to win two in a row; hit more career home runs than any shortstop in history (293) and more home runs in a single season (44) than any shortstop ever; elected to the Baseball Hall of Fame (1977).

One of the best teams in the Negro leagues at the time was the Kansas City Monarchs. Although there were a few black players in both the American League and National League by this time, a lot of great players were still playing in the Negro leagues. The Monarchs had Satchel Paige, who was later named to the Baseball Hall of Fame. A scout from the Monarchs saw Ernie playing for the Colts and was impressed. The scout signed Ernie for the 1950 season and, after graduating from high school the next spring, Ernie left Texas to join the Monarchs. He hit .255 with one homer in his first season. He was paid $300 per month.

At the end of the 1950 season, Ernie was drafted into the Army. Ernie, 19, was assigned to an anti-aircraft group and served in Germany for two years. There, he played baseball when he could and learned every position except catcher.

When he got out of the Army, Ernie rejoined the Monarchs. In 1953, his first year back with the team, he batted an astounding .380 and hit 23 home runs.

HERO'S HEROES: Ernie had a couple of heroes himself: St. Louis Cardinal star Stan Musial and Brooklyn Dodger legend Jackie Robinson. Ernie admired Stan as a great player and for his conduct on and off the field. He considered Jackie to be an ideal athlete and competitor and the most versatile player of his time.

Late that season, Tom Gordon, the business manager of the Chicago Cubs' farm team in Macon, Georgia, saw Ernie play in a game. He immediately phoned the Cubs' office to tell them about this outstanding young player he had spotted. The Cubs sent a group of their scouts to watch Ernie play and they were also very impressed.

The Cubs bought Ernie's contract from the Monarchs and brought him up to play with the Chicago club for the final 10 games of the 1953 season. Ernie hit .314 with two home runs in those 10 games and convinced the Cubs that he should be their starting shortstop for the 1954 season. It was only six years after he had played his first baseball game and Ernie was a big leaguer!

And he was an immediate star. In 1954, Ernie missed only one inning while playing in every one of the Cubs' 154 games. He hit .275 with 19 homers, and drove in 79 runs. In 1955, he blasted 44 home runs — the most ever hit by a shortstop — and was named to the N.L. All-Star team. Five of Ernie's homers that year came with the bases loaded!

WHEN Kirby Puckett was 10 years old in 1971, Ernie Banks was 40 and in his final season in professional baseball. He played in only 39 games for the Chicago Cubs and hit .193 while belting the last three of his 512 major league homers.

Ernie dominated the league from 1957 to 1960. He hit more than 40 home runs and drove in 100 or more runs in each of those seasons. Twice he led the league in homers and twice he was the RBI (runs batted in) leader, not to mention the two N.L. Most Valuable Player awards he won.

Ernie's home run statistics are amazing because he was not a big man physically. He stood 6' 1" but weighed only about 160 pounds. He got his power from his wrists and his forearms, which were very strong. He also used a very light bat, which helped him to swing the bat quickly.

Most home run hitters in the 1950's were strong men who used heavy bats that weighed 38 to 40 ounces. Ernie was one of the first players to use a light bat.

"Actually, Stan Musial [the Hall of Fame outfielder who

played for the St. Louis Cardinals] was the hitter who started the transition from heavy to light bats," said Ernie. "The way he was able to hit with power while maintaining a high batting average made everybody think and experiment.

"I went to the light bat partly by accident. I was standing by the batting cage at the old Polo Grounds one day and picked up a 31-ounce bat that [New York Giants star] Monte Irvin had acquired. I told Monte 'This feels good' and he told me I ought to use one like it.

"The next day I experimented with it in batting practice and the ball was jumping off the bat. I weighed only 160 pounds, but I could get terrific bat speed swinging that light wood. I hit only 19 home runs in 1954, but the next year I really took off. I hit five grand slams and a total of 44 homers. The light bat was my livelihood. It made me a better hitter."

Hitting was what Ernie was best known for. But he was also an accomplished fielder. During his 8½ seasons as the Cubs' shortstop, he led the N.L. in fielding percentage three times. In 1959, he had a major-league leading 519 assists while making only 12 errors, the fewest ever by a shortstop at that time. Ernie eventually switched from shortstop to first base because of knee problems.

ERNIE SAID: "You must try to generate your happiness within yourself. If you are not happy in one place, chances are you will not be happy any place."

After the 1971 season, Ernie retired at the age of 40. He had set records for hitting and for fielding and was named to 11 All-Star teams. Despite his many achievements as a player, though, Ernie never got the opportunity to play in a post-season game. One player doesn't make a team, no matter how good that player is, and the Cubs were not very good throughout most of Ernie's career. From Ernie's rookie year of 1954 through the 1966 season, the Cubs never finished higher than fifth. In the last five years of his career, they were competitive, finishing third in the N.L. twice. Then, when the league divisions were created in 1969, the Cubs finished second twice and third once in the N.L. East between 1969 and 1971.

To this day, Ernie holds the major-league record for the most games played (2,528) without playing in a post-season contest.

Ernie's career isn't only measured by his performance on the field, however. He was one of the most popular Cubs players ever. He was very active in Chicago community affairs and he spent much of his spare time working with youth groups.

> **OTHERS SAID:** "Ernie was . . . always enthusiastic. And he worked hard to make himself good. People don't realize that it didn't come that easy. He was always working." — *Gene Baker, Cubs second baseman and Ernie's roommate, on the eve of Ernie's election to the baseball Hall of Fame*

Throughout his career, Ernie was known for his very happy, friendly personality. He became known as "the Sunshine Kid" and "Mr. Cub" to the Chicago reporters. His love of the game of baseball always came shining through. He was well known for saying, "It's a beautiful day; let's play two."

That's quite a change from the little boy who didn't even want to play one!